DON'T SAY "I DO" UNTIL YO

- How much the "marriage penalty" adds to your income taxes
- How your potential spouse's debts can hurt you
- Why senior citizens may choose to cohabit, not marry
- What a new spouse's income can do to the eligibility for financial aid of college-age children from a previous marriage
- How a postmarital agreement can save your marriage and your assets during risky financial ventures
- What to do about the one-time exclusion of $125,000 from income taxes on the sale of a home—before you marry
- When stepparent adoption is a must
- What kind of lawyer can help couples protect their money and security best

THE MARRIAGE HANDBOOK
Be smart. Be safe. Be ready.

JOHNETTE DUFF is a practicing family law attorney. GEORGE G. TRUITT is a certified public accountant and certified financial planner. They are the authors of *The Spousal Equivalent Handbook: A Legal and Financial Guide to Living Together*, also available in a Plume edition.

Also by Johnette Duff, J.D.,
and George G. Truitt, C.P.A.

The Spousal Equivalent Handbook:
A Legal and Financial Guide to Living Together

The Marriage Handbook

A *legal and financial guide*
to your spousal rights

**Johnette Duff, J.D., and
George G. Truitt, C.P.A., C.F.P.**

A PLUME BOOK

PUBLISHER'S NOTE
This publication is designed to provide accurate and authoritative information in regard to the subject matter covered. It is sold with the understanding that the publisher is not engaged in rendering legal, accounting or other professional service. If legal advice or other expert assistance is required, the service of a competent professional person should be sought.

PLUME
Published by the Penguin Group
Penguin Books USA Inc., 375 Hudson Street, New York, New York 10014, U.S.A.
Penguin Books Ltd, 27 Wrights Lane, London W8 5TZ, England
Penguin Books Australia Ltd, Ringwood, Victoria, Australia
Penguin Books Canada Ltd, 10 Alcorn Avenue,
Toronto, Ontario, Canada M4V 3B2
Penguin Books (N.Z.) Ltd, 182–190 Wairau Road, Auckland 10, New Zealand

Penguin Books Ltd, Registered Offices: Harmondsworth, Middlesex, England

First published by Plume, an imprint of Dutton Signet,
a division of Penguin Books USA Inc.

First Printing, January, 1994
10 9 8 7 6 5 4 3 2 1

 REGISTERED TRADEMARK—MARCA REGISTRADA

LIBRARY OF CONGRESS CATALOGING-IN-PUBLICATION DATA
Duff, Johnette.
    The marriage handbook : a legal and financial guide to your
spousal rights / Johnette Duff and George G. Truitt.
        p.   cm.
    ISBN 0-452-27125-8
    1. Marriage law—United States.   2. Husband and wife—United
States.   3. Marital property—United States.   I. Truitt, George G.
II. Title.
KF510.D84   1994
346.7301′6—dc20   93-24042
[347.30616]   CIP

Printed in the United States of America
Set in Century Expanded

To Johnny & Dorothy Smith and L. G. & May Truitt,
who taught us about "till death do us part."
And to our "adopted" parents, Bill and Deanie Russell.
Happy 33rd!

CONTENTS

2: ACQUIRING PROPERTY 31

Marital Property • Separate or Community? • The Separate Property Theory • Marital versus Nonmarital Property • The Community Property Theory • Marital Debts • Marital Debts in Separate Property States • Marital Debts in Community Property States • Interstate Issues • Uniform Marital Property Act • Title to Property • Tenants in Common and Joint Tenants • Pitfalls • Don't Roll the Dice

3: TYING THE FISCAL KNOT 51

Dollars and Sense • To Pool or Not to Pool? • The Hidden Cost of Marriage • Duty of Support • Jay and Daisy • Pat and Mike • Yours, Mine, and Ours • Before You Tie the Knot . . .

4: ESTATE AND FINANCIAL PLANNING 65

Your Estate • Intestate Succession • Last Will and Testaments • Changing Your Will • Holographic and Joint Wills • Living Wills • Transferring Assets Outside Your Will • Living and Testamentary Trusts • Revocable Trusts • Irrevocable Trusts • Financial Planning • Set Goals and Objectives • Maintaining a Vital Papers File

5: MARITAL CONTRACTS 79

Who Needs Them? • What Goes in One? • Premarital Agreements • Advantages of Premarital Agreements • Public Institution or Private Relationship? • Elements of a Marital Contract • Pat and Mike • Postmarital Contracts • Now That I'm Convinced . . .

x   *Contents*

ACKNOWLEDGMENTS

Thanks must go to a number of people who have helped us. Jani Deters, for reading the manuscript in progress; Phil Morabito, whose unstinting support and indefatigable public relations efforts have led to appearances on "Today," "CBS This Morning," and coverage by *The Wall Street Journal*; to our editor, Michaela Hamilton, for "discovering" us and sticking with us while we shaped and reshaped this manuscript; to Kate Bandos for inviting us to the party in the first place; to our agent, Jonathan Dolger, and his able assistant, Carol-Ann Dearnaley, for championing our cause; and to Bernice Goodman, friend and running buddy, for her staunch and tireless encouragement and for having an unerring knack for finding the right restaurant.

AN INTRODUCTION TO MARRIAGE

By all means marry. If you get a good spouse, you'll become happy; if you get a bad one, you'll become a philosopher.   —Socrates

Obtaining a license to drive requires a course of study and a written test. Obtaining a license to marry requires no preparation. Consequently, couples about to marry know more about traffic laws than the marriage laws.

Saying "I do" launches a romantic new life together, but it also marks the beginning of a legal status replete with complex rules and obligations. No one warns the happy couple just how important a full understanding of their legal rights and duties can be. We intend to change that: this handbook will tell you all you need to know, and more than you ever expected, about the marriage laws and how to make them work for you, not against you.

THREE AT THE ALTAR

Romance doesn't need to obscure the practical considerations of marriage, but it's safe to say that the last thing on the mind of that blushing bride or nervous groom is the fact that the state (used in both the literal and generic sense, denoting any form of governmental authority) is at the altar, too. The vows a happy couple repeats are binding them to an unwritten contract of marriage, dictated not only by the laws of the federal government and their home state, but by prior court decisions and the all-too-human interpretations of these precedents by attorneys and judges.

Marriage, in reality, is a contract between three people: man, woman, and "state." The marriage contract and the laws behind it, many of which are based on outmoded assumptions, will affect the social, emotional, psychological, and economic life of a husband and wife. With the changing realities in our contemporary society, practical considerations must go hand in hand with love.

Until there is trouble in paradise, few realize the basic terms of the agreement they have entered. We've all been warned not to sign a contract without first reading it or seeking an attorney's advice. Those about to marry, however, have never been prepared for the fine print in their new contract.

Unfortunately, the lack of knowledge concerning the state's marriage contract is all too common among those who are about to become bound by its terms and conditions. Consequently, if this were any other contract, the husband or wife would have grounds to claim consumer fraud for lack of disclosure. If all of the terms were fully disclosed, who knows how many would sign on the dotted line without first negotiating a more personalized bargain?

Those couples who realize that there *are* legal and financial consequences that come with a marriage license are often victims of misinformation, of stories they have heard from friends about what the laws are and how these laws impact their lives. The lack of uniformity in state laws is an added complication. With our mobile society, couples might marry in one state, become bound by the laws of a new home state, and have no knowledge of the laws of either. Our intention is to fill this vacuum and shed light on the ramifications of the marital union—whether you are engaged or currently married, whether you are marrying for the first time or have walked down the aisle before.

DIFFERENT NEEDS, ONE OPTION

Surprisingly, although divorce laws have undergone drastic changes in this century, the marriage laws have remained relatively unchanged. Unfortunately, the legal regulation of marriage often does not reflect the realities of today's society. The American family has changed.

Reading these words are couples—

- Who are marrying for the first time
- Who are already married
- Who are veterans of any number of multiple marriages
- Who are living together and wondering if they should make it legal
- Who are bringing children to a marriage
- Who are both financially secure
- Who have vastly different economic situations
- Who have outstanding student loans, alimony, child support, tax obligations, or other consumer debts
- Who are twentysomething
- Who are baby boomers in their thirties and forties
- Who are in their fifties, sixties, or older
- Who are self-employed
- Who own family businesses
- Who have a commuter marriage
- Who married in one state but have moved to another

The list goes on and on.

The one form of marriage permitted under our laws remains the only option for couples who want a legal relationship, despite their age or former marital status, regardless of whether they have children or not, and despite their sexual orientation. The idea that marriage will last a lifetime is closely connected to the idea that marriage is for the young. In today's society, however, a bride and groom may not be young, and they may not be marrying for the first time.

Unfortunately, because couples considering marriage have many different needs, it is not uncommon for the laws that govern marriage to conflict with these needs. Couples considering a remarriage, senior citizens looking for companionship without legal complications, same-sex couples denied the right to marry, and fathers and mothers with ready-made families all seek answers from the same legal relationship. Too often, financial penalties come attached to the marriage license for these couples; in many cases, the price is too high.

Society's best interests are served by stable relationships, and marriage is undoubtedly the cornerstone of the family. Marriage offers emotional and spiritual benefits that may be lacking in a less committed relationship. There is little question that children benefit from marriage, both emotionally and legally. Until the laws begin to keep pace with the changing face of the American family, understanding the legal and financial implications of the laws that affect your individual situation must be each couple's responsibility.

SO WHAT DO I NEED TO KNOW?

Each state has different requirements that must be met before a couple may legally marry. These requisites vary throughout the country and are influenced by both state and federal laws. Although the regulation of marriage is determined by each state, these laws are zealously protected by federal constitutional protections. Finding out how to "get married" is the first step in the process of understanding the marriage contract.

Government regulation continues after marriage, defining the many rights and duties in the ongoing marital relationship. The most consequential of these regulations are the laws that determine how assets are owned or how debts must be paid both during the marriage and upon death of a spouse or dissolution of the relationship. Every state has different rules and interpretations regarding the property of husband and wife, although there are only two basic categories of marital property ownership in our country.

SEPARATE VERSUS COMMUNITY

The fifty states are divided into separate property and community property states. Unfortunately, that is the first and last generalization to be made about property laws in the United States. Within each state, the rules affecting property ownership vary widely. The two diverse theories are explained in general in chapter 2. Specifics of the laws of each state are included in Appendix A.

INHERITANCE LAWS

Also included in Appendix A are the intestate succession laws of the fifty states. When someone dies without a will, they have died intestate. Upon marriage, spouses acquire the right to inherit from each other automatically because the state determines the distribution of property to the surviving spouse under the laws of intestate succession.

An understanding of such statutes is crucial, particularly when there are children of the marriage or from a prior marriage. Some states have different provisions for children from a current marriage as opposed to children from a prior marriage, and this distinction can have important ramifications for a surviving spouse.

ESTATE PLANNING AND FINANCIAL ADVICE

After reviewing the intestate inheritance laws for your state, the importance of a valid will and estate planning for a married couple becomes evident. Practical advice on preparing a will is presented herein, along with information to help surviving spouses avoid unnecessary state and federal taxes, as well as the long delays and expense of the probate process.

OTHER MARITAL RIGHTS AND DUTIES

Although the ramifications of property ownership of husband and wife are arguably the most crucial factor in a marriage contract, there are many collateral considerations in the marital relationship. The variety of privileges and/or obligations that legal marriage conveys include the right to share in pension and retirement benefits, the right to an "insurable interest" in the other's life, the obligation to support a spouse, the question of a name change for a new wife, the ramifications of choosing a state for legal residency of a marriage, and concerns about children. Important as well are privileged communications between spouses, the right to sue for loss of consortium, and last but not least, tax ramifications.

TAX CONSEQUENCES OF MARRIAGE

The impact of state and federal tax laws is one of the most overlooked aspects of the marital relationship. The "marriage penalty tax" today is a reality for many two-income couples, but planning ahead for the extra tax bite is rarely part of the pre-wedding preparation. The crunch of higher taxes probably won't, and probably shouldn't, deter couples from walking down the aisle. However, the realities of the Internal Revenue Code and corresponding state regulations must be considered when discussing the legal and financial ramifications of marriage.

MARITAL AGREEMENTS

In the past few years, premarital contracts have received much controversial coverage in the press. Even those who oppose the idea of an "unromantic" premarital agreement, however, should realize that they are committing to a contract from the state.

The idea, and the ideal, is to make the marriage laws work for you. Often, it isn't until the death of a spouse or dissolution of a relationship that couples find that their fate is determined by the state-controlled marriage regulations.

The basic premise of this book is that you can structure a marriage, within the laws of your state, that meets the special requirements of your particular situation. Your marriage is different from everyone else's: maybe your marriage contract should be, too.

CONSIDER MODIFYING THE STATE'S CONTRACT

Making the law work for you often means fashioning your own marriage contract. Any such agreement will be upheld unless it contravenes basic state ideas on how a marriage should be structured. Within certain boundaries, adding your own agreement to the state's contract can help ensure that your marriage is a life-long partnership that works for both husband and wife.

Although changes in our society in the past few decades have meant the constant reevaluation of our family laws, contemporary changes in the marital relationship are not a new phenomenon. The institution has survived many crises and permutations through the ages. As an early form of social organization, marriage has always been linked to the survival of society itself and has throughout the ages been regulated by the powers that be.

Changes in society, however, too often outpace changes in our laws. Today, couples are surprised to find that their relationship is bound by old-fashioned assumptions about the family—assumptions that have no basis in the reality of today's society. No matter how distasteful this control is, our intimate personal relationships are regulated by duties and responsibilities determined by the legislatures and the courts.

CAN THIS BOOK HELP EVERYONE?

Our overview of marriage raises issues most brides and grooms, or husbands and wives, have never considered. *The Marriage Handbook*, however, is not intended as a substitute for professional advice. Variations in the laws of the fifty states and the infinite number of issues facing couples about to walk down the aisle make a do-it-yourself guide impossible.

We do guarantee that you will be forewarned, henceforth forearmed, in these pages about potential pitfalls that could impact your relationship. Knowing your rights and obligations is the first step. Professional assistance is the second one. Preventive measures are less expensive and more successful than emergency procedures.

Don't hesitate to take that second step if your situation warrants it. Applying the information herein to your personal situation may very likely require the assistance of an attorney, an accountant, or other professionals familiar with applicable state and federal laws (as well as the local rules and customs of the courts in the county or parish where you live).

FOR BETTER OR FOR WORSE?

Our account of marriage is designed to help you beat the high cost of love colliding with the law. Married couples can attest to the fact that a life together, although offering less tangible rewards, encompasses enormous practical problems. Someone has to pay the rent, pay the car insurance, make sure the medical coverage is current, and so on. Love doesn't blind married couples to such a degree that they can't keep the lights and the phone turned on. So why should it overshadow the legal and financial ramifications of the marital union?

Determining if and how you can improve on the contract the state hands you at the altar means writing your own final chapter. The institution of marriage looks like it's going to last. We hope the information in these pages will add similar staying power to your relationship.

Chapter 1

HOW TO GET MARRIED

Keep your eyes wide open before marriage, half shut afterward.
                                    —Benjamin Franklin

- Are you old enough to obtain a marriage license in your state?
- Are you related in any way to your potential spouse?
- Are you in the Armed Forces?
- Do you have final divorce papers from any prior marriage?
- Is there any physical or mental reason why you could not legally marry based on the laws of your state?
- Do you live in a state that recognizes common-law marriage?

The power to determine who can marry in the United States has traditionally been the exclusive power of each state. The special nature of the rights, duties, and privileges of the marriage contract stem from the role of the state in encouraging marriage.

Still, the assumption that everyone has a right to marry is limited by the state legislature's determination of each person's capacity to enter a valid marriage. Each state has substantive requirements that relate to the ability to marry. Restrictions on the right to marry are based on such considerations as—

- Family relationships
- Heterosexuality
- Monogamy
- Health
- Age

The state also controls solemnization procedures and determines the ability of a party to understand and consent to a marriage. Justifications for these regulations and requirements include:

- Promotion of public health
- Protection of public morality
- Eugenics (the science that deals with heredity)
- Promotion of family stability

Some commentators argue that there are too few requirements, too halfheartedly enforced. On the other hand, critics of state regulation believe the reasoning behind many of the laws to be ambiguous and archaic, and seek to limit the state involvement that does exist.

CONSTITUTIONAL LIMITATIONS

Because marriage is protected by the Constitution, state laws dealing with marriage are subject to certain limitations. In the past, courts have defined marriage both as a constitutionally protected basic civil right and as a fundamental freedom.

The Bill of Rights, the first ten amendments to our Constitution, set forth the many rights and freedoms we sometimes take for granted. Embodied in the Fourteenth Amendment is equal protection under the law for all citizens and due process of law, two concepts that have impacted American marriage in a variety of ways, as we will see throughout this chapter.

FEDS 4, STATES 0

In this century, there have been state prohibitions on marriage that have been struck down by the federal government. Examples include:

- Antimiscegenation statutes that sought to prevent mixed race marriage

- A law that required a father with a child support obligation ordered by a court to obtain that court's permission to remarry

- A school board regulation that did not allow married students to participate in extracurricular activities

- A United States Merchant Marine Academy regulation that prohibited cadets from marrying before graduation

FEDS 0, STATES 3

However, the states have also placed limitations on marriage that have withstood constitutional scrutiny. These include:

- Laws prohibiting polygamy

- A law that prohibited the marriage of a felon sentenced to life imprisonment

- Denial of marriage rights to same-sex couples

THE MARRIAGE LICENSE AND CEREMONY

Fifty states have enacted fifty different scenarios before a couple can enter into the legal contract of marriage. Yet all fifty states agree that a marriage license and a formal recordation of the marriage are required.

The actual licensing authority varies from state to state: it may be a county clerk or a justice of the peace. The license is usually issued in the county where the marriage will be performed. A man and woman applying for a marriage license must reveal personal information related to their capacity to enter a marriage to the licensing authority. Many states also require a physical examination as part of the application process, and a waiting period between application and actual issuance of the license.

The purpose of this delay, or "cooling off" period, is to thwart hasty marriages. The time period prescribed by state statutes ranges anywhere from twenty-four hours to five days.

State statutes also designate persons qualified to solemnize a wedding ceremony, including certain civil officers and church leaders. The form of the ceremony itself is not prescribed by statute, but minimum requirements include:

- Consent to the marriage (I do)
- A declaration of the status of husband and wife (I now pronounce you husband and wife)

The license and the ceremony serve the purpose of providing objective proof that the marriage took place, avoiding the problems of proof and fraud that might arise in an informal, or common-law, marriage situation (which will be discussed in detail later in this chapter).

The states vary in their statutory rules regarding licensing and ceremony; the provisions may be classified as—

- Mandatory (the marriage does not legally exist without them)
- Advisory (where noncompliance is possibly punishable by fine, but the marriage itself is valid)

The specific requirements to obtain a marriage license in your state are listed in Appendix A.

AGE

The question of the age of the parties entering a marriage relationship has been the subject of more legislative regulation than any other issue. Attempting to promote marital stability and maturity, states have cited the high divorce rate among couples married between the ages of fifteen and nineteen (approximately three times higher than those who are out of their teens) as the logic behind these laws. Criticism of these requirements stresses that the laws can be circumvented if the parties travel to a state whose requirements meet their needs or simply live in nonmarital cohabitation when the state thwarts their desire to marry.

Much of our justice system in the United States today is based on the unwritten "common law" of England. The basic theory behind common law is that justice is based on the social needs of the community and adapts to new conditions as required. The common law rule in England was that marriage could not take place until there was an ability to procreate, usually set at about age twelve for females and fourteen for males.

Common law age requirements were not structured to encourage equal protection of the sexes under the law. The older age for boys was considered necessary because it was felt that they needed education and training before marriage; women did not. The impact of this inequality, a tradition still reflected in the laws of some states, has been twofold.

First, because the husband was older than the wife, he was the head of the household, with the wife playing a subordinate role. Second, the younger age requirements led women to believe that early marriage was encouraged. The earlier the marriage, the earlier a woman started a family, limiting her opportunities for education and further training. Many jurisdictions have declared such laws unconstitutional because of a denial of equal protection under the law.

In an attempt to promote uniformity among the states, the National Conference of Commissioners on Uniform State Laws has proposed a variety of laws that affect marriage, including the Uniform Marriage and Divorce Act (UMDA), the Uniform Marital Property Act, and the Uniform Premarital Agreement Act. Some states have adopted these uniform laws, and some states have adopted similar laws.

The UMDA sets age eighteen as the age of consent for both sexes. It also would require those under age eighteen but over age sixteen to obtain parental consent, and those under age sixteen to obtain both parental and judicial consent.

The UMDA has sought to favor greater access to the status of marriage, arguing that society favors the institution over an illicit relationship. The American Bar Association approved the provisions of the UMDA in 1974. The argument over the age of consent to marry may become moot, though. The trend among the young, as documented by the Census Bureau, is to postpone marriage to pursue college educations and careers.

CONSANGUINITY AND AFFINITY

Consanguinity describes a blood relationship or descent from a common ancestor. Affinity describes a relationship based on marriage. Rules regarding marriage between those who are closely related by blood or marriage exist in every state.

Taboos against incest have existed in all societies. A distinction may be made between parent-child or brother-sister incest as opposed to "legal" incest regulated by the marriage laws, such as first cousin relationships or relationships with adopted children.

There are several reasons for incest prohibitions. First, affinity restrictions are based on the religious idea that a husband and wife become one flesh and are therefore related by blood to the relatives of the other.

Eugenics is a second reason, with the concern that inbreeding leads to defective offspring. Although all states prohibit marriages between the full and half blood in a direct line of ascent or descent, the pros and cons of the argument in prohibiting marriages between first cousins have led to almost a 50/50 split among the state laws. Proponents point out that Abraham Lincoln and Charles Darwin were the children of first-cousin marriages; opponents cite such situations as a 1910 Washington state court decision that voided the marriage of two first cousins, pointing out that their only offspring was "deaf and dumb."

A third reason for prohibiting marriages based on consanguinity and affinity is primarily sociological. In the past, seeking a mate outside the family unit led to alliances between families, which could be necessary for survival during time of upheaval in society. Also, preventing sexual rivalries in a family made the unit more stable and productive.

Adoption and illegitimacy further complicate this issue. Illegitimacy does not change the prohibitions against consanguinity. The inclusion of those related by adoption, however, is a sociological issue, not a biological one. Obviously, adoption does not eliminate the ties between an adopted child and his biological relatives, but there have been arguments both for and against an adopted child's legal status within an adopted family.

The UMDA prohibits "marriages between ascendants and descendants, between siblings related by adoption, and between aunt and nephew and uncle and niece." It does not bar first cousin marriages, and this has been a continuing area of controversy. It also does not include prohibitions on marriages between those related by affinity.

MISCEGENATION

Miscegenation has been defined as the intermarrying, cohabiting, or interbreeding of persons of mixed races. The case of Loving vs. The State of Virginia (United States Supreme Court, 1967, 388 US 1) limited state regulation of the individual's right to choose a spouse.

In this case, a state statute prohibiting interracial marriage was found to violate the equal protection and due process clauses of the Fourteenth Amendment. The court found that "The Fourteenth Amendment requires that the freedom of choice to marry not be restricted by invidious racial discrimination."

In 1967, when this case was decided, sixteen states had miscegenation statutes on the books. Children of these marriages in states with such prohibitions had always been considered illegitimate.

The laws against such relationships began with the slave trade in the colonies. Coupled with the acquisition of Indian lands and the migration of Orientals, many states saw fit to enact laws against mixed marriages. There was no uniformity in the bias against racial groups. In the past, Mongolians, Hindus, Chinese, Japanese, Ethiopians, Malayans, and American Indians were all discriminated against by one state statute or another.

Arguments for preventing interracial marriage included Biblical accounts of the sin certain Israelites committed against God when they took "strange wives" from neighboring non-Jewish tribes. At common law, prohibitions against marriage with "persons of inferior ranks" also existed, adding justification to these prohibitions.

The Loving case overrode all arguments, and the federal government succeeded in repealing these laws. Similar discrimination still exists today, however, based on sexual orientation.

SAME-SEX MARRIAGE

Although prohibitions against interracial marriage were overturned less than twenty-five years ago, the state today still prohibits the marriage of a couple of the same sex. Two arguments are used to justify this position.

First, the law has always defined marriage as the union between a man and a woman. Second, there is the contention that marriage is a unique institution, designed for the procreation and rearing of children.

Many same-sex couples, faced with this prohibition and the AIDS crisis, have begun holding "bonding" ceremonies, replete with many traditional accoutrements of marriage. Although these ceremonies have no legal status, they are a creative response to the denial of the rights and duties of the marriage contract.

The denial of legal rights to these couples smacks of the same denial of equal protection as the miscegenation laws. Perhaps the legal establishment would be more comfortable with a change in semantics. The legal right to form a union of a same-sex couple does not have to be called "marriage." Laws giving these couples similar rights and duties, but with a different name, might satisfy this extremely controversial issue.

BIGAMY

The generally accepted Anglo-Saxon tradition has been that a person is allowed only one spouse at a time. Bigamy is the crime of contracting a second marriage while the first marriage is still in existence.

The state laws against bigamy vary. In some states, it is possible that bigamous cohabitation or common-law marriage could support charges of bigamy. In most cases, a divorce or annulment from one state will be recognized by any other, but often legal procedures may not have been finalized, complicating the question of a valid remarriage. In many states, there is a time limitation after divorce when another marriage may not be contracted.

"Quickie" divorces, such as those obtained in Mexico or the Dominican Republic, are another issue. Did the foreign court have jurisdiction to grant a divorce? Did one spouse acquire resident status in the country, even if only for the purpose of the divorce?

If one spouse challenges a quickie divorce, the courts may declare it invalid. Even if the divorce itself is recognized, the provisions regarding property and children may not be upheld. Or, on the flip side, if one spouse carries on as if accepting the divorce and later tries to challenge it, it may be too late. If you have any concerns about your marital status and are considering remarriage, consult an attorney in your home state.

POLYGAMY

Although many nomadic tribes, Old Testament patriarchs, and other successful cultures have permitted polygamy (the practice of having more than one spouse at a time), our society has refused to endorse the practice. At common law, there was no prohibition against polygamy until 1604.

Our federal government became involved in legislation on this issue because of the controversy over the Mormon Church when it officially adopted polygamy as a religious practice in 1852. This led to the case of Reynolds vs. United States (United States Supreme Court, 1878, 98 US 145).

Reynolds, a practicing Mormon, maintained that his religious beliefs justified breaking the law. The Supreme Court ruled that although Congress could not hinder freedom of religion, it could pass laws against polygamy because the practice was subversive to social order. In 1882, the Edmunds Anti-Polygamy Act further restricted the practice. In 1889, the Mormon Church itself declared that polygamy was forbidden and the furor died down.

MENTAL CAPACITY

The consent of both parties to enter a marriage contract was crucial for a valid marriage under common law. Today, all states have laws dealing with this issue of mental competence to consent to a marriage. These laws are based on the perceived duty to protect the incompetent person from legal responsibility that he or she might not understand.

Such statutes have not escaped criticism, in part because of their use of terms such as *idiots*, *imbeciles*, *feebleminded*, and *insane*. Such appellations make enforcement inconsistent and ambiguous. Some states have used the phrase "persons incapable of consenting to marriage from want of understanding," which, unfortunately, might encompass a wide range of our society.

There are arguments that such laws are discriminatory. In 1976 the President's Committee on Mental Retardation compiled a report that supported the right of differently abled people to marry and raise children, supporting the position that a denial of the right flies in the face of the Fourteenth Amendment.

PHYSICAL CAPACITY

State licensing statutes, annulment statutes, and divorce statutes all deal with the physical capacity of the parties to enter into a marriage contract by requiring that potential spouses be free of disease and physically capable of consummating a marriage.

Impotence has long been recognized as grounds for annulment of a marriage. The general definition of impotence is the inability to have normal sexual intercourse, due to any number of causes, whether mental or physical. Many jurisdictions require that this be a permanent condition. Concealment of a known condition of impotence may be grounds for fraud, which could void the marriage contract.

Sterility is not included in this definition of impotence. Sexual performance, not fertility, is the true test. Impotence after consummation of the marriage is not enough to void the union.

There are certain other physical conditions or diseases that might prohibit persons from marrying due to licensing procedures that require a medical examination or a blood test. Some states provide grounds for annulment for certain diseases. The most common diseases in question include venereal diseases, epilepsy, tuberculosis, and alcoholism or other drug addiction. As with many of the restrictions on marriage, these prohibitions have seen their share of criticism.

FRAUD

Voluntary consent is essential for a valid marriage contract. One of the grounds for annulment of a marriage in many states is fraud in the inducement of the marriage contract. Examples where fraud has been held to relate to the very essentials of a marriage are:

- Concealed pregnancy by another man
- Concealment of venereal disease
- Undisclosed sterility

Examples of misrepresentations that have not been upheld as fraud are:

- Lack of chastity
- Undisclosed prior marriage and divorce
- Previous bad character

PRISONERS

In the United States, a convicted criminal is subject to sanctions that limit or end many of his or her civil rights. In some states, the right to marry is one of them.

There is no uniform position among the states on the issue of a prisoner's right to take a spouse. The majority of states, however, do allow prisoners to marry.

ARMED FORCES

There are military regulations concerning the right of an enlisted man to enter a marriage. Before World War II, the armed forces did not regulate the marriage of soldiers in any way. In 1942, however, the War Department issued requirements that all overseas servicemen must obtain permission from their commanders before marrying.

Army Regulation 600-240, Marriage in Overseas Commands, requires that military personnel "obtain written approval from the senior area commander of their particular branch of the service before marrying." This is often seen as an infringement on the serviceman's rights and privileges as a citizen of the United States.

Proponents argue that the rules are justified because they prevent violation of immigration laws and discourage impetuous marriages. The arguments against include the point that an administrative body is contravening laws of the legislature and the rights under Loving vs. Virginia of a U.S. citizen to marry a person of another race, which is often the case when our armed forces are overseas. Despite criticism, the armed forces continue to regulate the right to marry.

NATIVE AMERICANS

The power to regulate marriage within a state is subject to certain restrictions by the federal government, as we have seen. One of these regulations not previously mentioned is the guarantee of the autonomy of the American Indian. "Indian customs" surrounding marriage are not subject to many state restrictions on marriage.

Indian traditions often include marriage without the benefit of clergy, and divorce by the unilateral action of one party. Both state and federal courts usually uphold these practices, and exempt Indians from following the same state and federal laws that relate to other citizens. Indian marriages are not regarded as common-law marriages, with the accompanying problems of proof, but as full ceremonial marriages.

VOID MARRIAGES

A void marriage is a marriage that never existed under the law. Because the law does not recognize the relationship, no dissolution of such a union is necessary. Examples include the following:

- Incest

  DENNIS and Brenda are first cousins from California. They marry in Arizona in 1993. Although their marriage would be recognized in their home state, their marriage is void because Arizona prohibits legal marriages between cousins.

- Prior undissolved marriage

  BART and Alice marry in Texas in 1990. Bart was formerly married in Louisiana, where his wife served him with a divorce petition in 1978. Bart never responded to the petition and assumed his wife finalized the divorce. In fact, she was unable to pay her attorney and the divorce was never granted. Bart and

Alice's marriage is void because Bart is still legally married to his wife in Louisiana.

Many states also have a waiting period after a divorce before a new marriage may be contracted, so it is important to be aware of such limitations before remarrying. However, the law does recognize that a party in a void marriage may be unaware of such impediments. The courts will protect what it terms a "putative" spouse; that is, a party who, in good faith, entered into what they believed to be a valid marriage. Protections include:

- The right to inherit
- The right to a property division
- Legitimacy of children
- The right to seek child support

VOIDABLE MARRIAGES

A voidable marriage is a marriage that is technically invalid but might later be made valid by an act of the parties. A voidable marriage may be ended by either annulment or divorce. Failure to annul the marriage upon knowledge of the impediment to the marriage may cause a party to lose their right to an annulment. Examples include the following:

- Marriages before the age of consent

    TAMLYN, seventeen, and Akira, eighteen, were married in Las Vegas after Tamlyn lied about her age. This marriage is voidable because she is underage. When her parents find out, they bring her home and have the marriage annulled. If Tamlyn's parents later consented to the marriage, or if the couple had continued to live together until she reached age eighteen, the marriage would have been valid.

- Marriages obtained by fraud or force

  HAROLD and Margaret are both in their sixties. Margaret has been financially secure since the death of her first husband, so she has Harold sign a premarital agreement before they marry. After the wedding, Harold realizes that Margaret isn't going to support him in the style he expected. Because he admits to her that he was only looking for a meal ticket, Margaret is able to obtain an annulment based on fraud.

- Marriage with a person of unsound mind (which, in some states, includes lack of capacity due to influence of alcohol or drugs)

- Marriage when either party is incapable of consummating the marriage

- Marriage entered into as a jest or a dare

- Marriage when one party has a loathsome disease unknown to the other

FOREIGN MARRIAGES

What about a foreign marriage? In a legal sense, "foreign" refers to either another state or another country. Under the "full faith and credit" doctrine, it is possible to legally marry in a location outside your home state because your state recognizes and respects the marriage laws of other states and countries.

If you want to get married in Las Vegas, or by a captain at sea, or on a secluded beach in the Caribbean, if the marriage is valid in the state or country in which it is performed, the union is valid in your state. (The only caveat might be a marriage that is "odious" in the eyes of a state; that is, marrying your brother or having six wives might be okay in some cultures, but don't push your luck.)

COMMON-LAW MARRIAGE

It is also important to be aware of the laws regarding informal, or common-law, marriage that remain on the books today if you live in a state that still recognizes this relationship.

Informal marriages in our country began with the early settlers in America. Long distances and inadequate roads between communities made finding someone to conduct a marriage ceremony and somewhere to record proof of the marriage difficult. An alternative to ceremonial marriage was necessary, so the legal recognition of informal, or common-law, marriages became widespread. When competent parties agreed to form a relationship and live together as husband and wife without a ceremony, the law adapted to acknowledge that a marriage had been created, conveying the same legal status and consequences on the parties as if a public solemnization and recording had taken place.

As the colonies prospered, the public became better educated and less hampered by transportation problems. The need for "proof" of the intentions of the parties in informal relationships and the possibility of fraudulent claims led many states away from the trend of common-law marriages.

Gradually, governments began to deny the right of two people to determine their own form of "marriage." Any alternative to ceremonial marriage began to be viewed as an attempt to undermine the stability of marriage and family life. Eventually, the courts and legislatures in the majority of the states took the position that only traditional families should be promoted by the laws and passed laws outlawing common-law marriage. Today, only fourteen states and the District of Columbia still recognize informal, or common-law, marriage. Ohio repealed its law in 1992, but the following states still recognize this relationship:

- Alabama
- Colorado
- Georgia
- Idaho

- Iowa
- Kansas
- Montana
- New Hampshire
- Oklahoma
- Pennsylvania
- Rhode Island
- South Carolina
- Texas
- Utah
- The District of Columbia

What is the result of a common-law marriage? Consider the following example:

JOHN and Jane begin living together in 1980 in a state that recognizes common-law marriage. They stay together for twelve years, file joint income tax returns, and sign a lease to an apartment with Jane using John's last name. In 1992, John marries someone else and locks Jane out of the apartment. Jane immediately sues for divorce, telling John she will have him charged with bigamy. Subsequently, the court tells John his new marriage is invalid because he is legally married to Jane and orders John to vacate the apartment, where Jane will be allowed to live until further hearing on the divorce.

Other states will recognize an informal marriage between two people if it was originally contracted in one of the states previously listed. The rationalization for retaining the legal status of common-law marriage has been the protection of children, as many states did not recognize paternity suits until forced to by the Supreme Court in 1973. Before that time, terming a relationship a marriage was the only way the states could order fathers to support their offspring.

Even the states that continue to recognize informal marriage can be critical of this legal anachronism. In the past, society afforded this protection to those on the lower rungs of the socioeconomic ladder. In our changing times, those who really need protection are those on the higher rungs of that ladder who, for whatever reason, haven't formalized their union and have the deep pockets to make a lawsuit worth fighting.

Celebrities seem to be the ones who focus media attention on such issues and bring them to the attention of the public. In the past few years, actor William Hurt and major league baseball's Dave Winfield have been slapped with claims of common-law marriage, making people aware that this is not an outmoded idea whose time has come and gone.

A common misconception is that the length of cohabitation creates common-law status. This is not true: there must be an agreement between the parties to be married and a "holding-out" (representing yourself as husband and wife) in the community before this legal fiction is created. This agreement does not have to be in writing, and can be implied from the behavior of the parties. Signing leases as husband and wife or filing joint tax returns are examples of proof a court could use to imply an agreement. Appendix A explains the laws that exist in your home state.

If you are concerned that your situation may have created an informal marriage, contact an attorney. If you have complied with the requirements, the law is clear. A common-law marriage is the full equivalent of a ceremonial marriage, and a divorce is required to dissolve the relationship.

NOW THAT YOU QUALIFY . . .

With the requirements to enter a legal marital contract explained, an understanding of the legal and financial duties and obligations of the ongoing marital union logically follows. The changes of the past twenty years have redefined marriage to such an extent that an understanding of the rights and obligations that accompany the marriage license is critical. Modern romance often calls for significant compromise. The secret is to learn to make the existing laws work *for* you, not against you. Without knowledge of the applicable rules of the game, the odds of failure increase. Why gamble?

Chapter 2

ACQUIRING PROPERTY

*I am a marvelous housekeeper. Every time I leave
a man I keep his house.*   —Zsa Zsa Gabor

- Do you live in a community property or separate property state?

- Do any of the assets you own prior to marriage have the potential to produce income; such as rental property, interest on investments, or future profits from business deals?

- Do you or your potential spouse bring any significant debts to the relationship?

The complexities and the subtleties of the property rights that come with a marriage license should require a course of study and a written test. Knowledge and communication about the prudent management of your marital assets can only avoid misunderstandings and conflict during your marriage. All married couples should be aware of the laws in their home state and how their property is affected by these laws.

Any discussion of marital property, unfortunately, must also

include the "worst-case scenario" of division of property upon
dissolution of a marriage. As any discussion of estate planning
and wills deals with topics most would rather avoid, understanding the rights and obligations of marriage can often only be addressed by a discussion of how property would be apportioned
between the spouses in the event of a breakup, as many of our
examples illustrate. Our goal is not to help you plan for divorce,
but rather to help you protect property rights in your marriage
that could be adversely affected by these laws.

MARITAL PROPERTY

Marital property includes all assets acquired by either husband or wife during a marriage, such as:

- Wages from employment
- Home furnishings
- Motor vehicles
- Stocks, bonds, annuities, and dividends
- Pension plans and retirement benefits
- Animals
- Insurance policies
- Interests in vacation homes or timeshares
- Bank accounts and the interest on them
- Business interests, including copyrights, patents, goodwill,
  and so on
- Personal injury or workers' compensation awards
- Promissory notes
- Tax refunds
- *Debts* (too often forgotten in a discussion of marital
  property)

SEPARATE OR COMMUNITY?

One question must be answered before ownership of assets within a marriage can be determined: Do you live in a separate property or a community property state?

The fifty states are divided into separate property and community property states. However, each state has enacted statutes that affect your property in different ways. The following general information is supplemented with the specific material for your home state included under "Property Distribution" in Appendix A.

THE SEPARATE PROPERTY THEORY

A total of forty-one states and the District of Columbia apply the theory of English common law to marital property ownership. The basic premise of this concept is that property and income acquired either before or during marriage belongs to the spouse who acquired it. The basis of the separate property laws was the male-dominated English tradition that a wife, being a mere possession herself, had no claim on property acquired during marriage.

In the past, the result of this tradition was that a homemaker without an outside job or assets in her own name could be financially destitute if her husband decided he wanted out of the marriage. Following the tradition of common law, the laws have adapted to the changes of society. Today, either by statute or by court decision, all of the separate property states apply the theory of "equitable distribution" to the division of property upon divorce.

MARITAL VERSUS NONMARITAL PROPERTY

Unless a couple has a written agreement, the actual title to property no longer controls who would own the property upon dissolution of the marriage. After considering the mitigating factors in each individual situation, the courts today have the power to determine whether an asset is marital or nonmarital (or separate) property in accordance with the statutes, as outlined in Appendix A for each state.

Many states, by statute, specifically *exclude* from their definition of marital property any property classified otherwise in a valid marital agreement. Property also excluded from the definition of marital property by these statutes *can*, but does not necessarily, include:

- Any separate property acquired prior to marriage

- Any separate property acquired by gift during marriage

- Any separate property acquired by inheritance during marriage

- Any increase in the foregoing separate property categories that is not a result of the efforts of the non-owner spouse

- A workers' compensation claim or personal injury claim (or similar legal award) for any degree of permanent disability or future medical payments awarded during the marriage

- Any asset purchased with separate property funds from the foregoing categories

Property not excluded from the definition of marital property is classified as marital property in a separate property state. Generalizations about the determination of ownership of these assets upon divorce are difficult to make, but potential considerations applied by the courts to an equitable division can include:

- Length of marriage
- Age, health, and station in life of parties
- The contribution of each spouse to the acquisition of the marital property, including the contribution of spouse as homemaker
- The occupation or vocational skills of the parties
- The amount and sources of income of the parties
- Estate, liabilities, and needs of each party and opportunity of each for further acquisition of capital assets and income
- The federal income tax consequences of the court's division of the property
- Value of the property set apart to each spouse
- Economic circumstances of each spouse at the time of the effective division of property, including the desirability of awarding the family home or right to live therein to the spouse with custody of the children
- Any increases or decreases in the value of the separate property of the spouse during marriage
- The depletion of the separate property for marital purposes in the past
- Prior marriage or obligations arising from a prior marriage
- The contribution of each of the parties in the acquisition and appreciation of the estate
- Whether the property award is in lieu of or in addition to alimony
- Debts of the parties
- Retirement benefits, including but not limited to social security, civil service, military, and railroad retirement benefits
- Property brought to the marriage by each party
- Direct or indirect contribution to education or career advancement by one party to the other

- The extent to which the efforts of one spouse have limited or decreased the other's earning power
- Difficulty of evaluating any asset or interest
- Wasteful dissipation of assets
- Transfer of assets without fair consideration
- The liquidity or nonliquidity of assets
- The conduct of the parties as to the cause of divorce to determine a distribution

Wise management of assets after marriage may include keeping nonmarital property separate from marital property and/or keeping accurate records of nonmarital funds used to benefit the marriage. In most situations, one spouse has no claim on the nonmarital assets of the other when ownership is undisputed.

However, the duty to support owed by one spouse to the other (discussed in greater detail in the next chapter) could possibly require the use of nonmarital property during or after a marriage if assets in the marital estate have been depleted. Consider the following situation:

CARL and Carol were married in 1987. Carol drops out of college to start a family, planning to return at a later date. Carl, who comes from a wealthy family, pursues a career as a dentist. Unfortunately, Carl's standard of living exceeds the income from his practice. After the birth of their third child, Carol returns to night school to finish her degree. Carl, meanwhile, has made several risky investments with his earnings in a futile attempt to support his excesses, which include fancy cars and gambling. When the financial pressure ends their marriage in 1992, Carol learns they have no marital assets. The court awards Carol a portion of Carl's income from family investments.

The only blanket statement that can be made about the determination of marital property is that the decision-making process can be taken away from the spouses and left to the caprices of the law. This holds true in community property states as well. Even the simple community property system of "you get half, I get half" has been complicated by modern legislation.

THE COMMUNITY PROPERTY THEORY

The community property theory began with the idea that everything accumulated during marriage from the labor of either spouse belonged equally to both husband and wife (although many states originally gave the husband the right to manage and control all community property). Most of the states with this theory were heavily influenced by Spain, who borrowed the concept from a nomadic tribe called the Visigoths. This accounts for the deviation from the common law of England, the tradition followed in the majority of the states. The community property states are:

- Arizona
- California
- Idaho
- Louisiana
- New Mexico
- Nevada
- Texas
- Washington
- Wisconsin (actually in a category by itself: see "Uniform Marital Property Act")

All property acquired during marriage in these states is considered community property unless a spouse can "rebut the presumption." This idea is similar to being innocent until proven guilty; that is, an asset is community property unless someone can prove to a court's satisfaction that it isn't.

Each state has created its own twists on the basic community property theory, and these interpretations can impact significantly on a married couple. Accurate records or a written agreement acquire a certain importance in many situations. For example, in community property states, a spouse may own what is classified as "separate property" if—

- The property was owned before marriage
- The property was acquired by gift during the marriage
- The property was inherited during the marriage

However, separate property "commingled" with community property complicates the characterization of the property, making it difficult to determine if it falls under column A, Separate Property, or column B, Community Property. Examples of commingling would include separate property funds used to help pay for a home purchased after marriage or money deposited into a joint account, as in the following scenario:

NICOLE and Geoffrey were married for twenty years and have three children. Nicole was a secretary when she married, but did not work outside the home after the children came. Geoffrey has had a mid-life crisis: he has moved out and served Nicole with divorce papers, telling her he is in love with another woman whom he intends to marry.

Nicole at first believes that she will have the substantial inheritances from her parents and grandparents as a cushion for herself and the children. Under the law, her attorney explains, those assets should be "her" money. However, the funds were deposited in a joint account with the profits from Geoffrey's business. It is impossible to tell if the funds remaining are the community property profits from the business or the separate property from Nicole's inheritance.

In a situation such as this, if the parties have not kept the funds separate or executed a written agreement, it is virtually impossible for a judge to determine what belongs to Geoffrey and what belongs to Nicole. The judge's job is much easier if he declares that the character of the inheritance has changed—Nicole obviously intended the separate property funds from her inheritance as a gift to the community account.

This is a very likely result. But is it a fair result? Geoffrey's business is booming; Nicole missed the computer revolution and doesn't know her way around a modern office. She could really use the money, but she can't prove that she meant to keep the inheritance separate. Why? Because she was not aware of the law and took no measures to protect her separate property from such a frustrating finale.

If Nicole had used the money to buy herself a new car titled only in her name, there would have been no problem. Such a transaction is simple—the money easily traceable to her separate funds. In most cases, a material possession takes the character of the property used to acquire it.

What if Nicole had deposited the money in her name alone, then used the funds for a down payment on a house purchased during the marriage as a community property investment? In such a situation, she would be entitled to *reimbursement*, a legal theory used to justify a monetary award when separate property funds have been used to increase the value of community assets. Showing that separate property funds were used to purchase a community property asset entitles a spouse to a return on the investment, as long as the community asset retains sufficient value to pay the spouse back.

Yet another modern complication of the community property theory is: how does your state treat the issue of income from separate property? Some states consider income from separate property to be community property, as in the following scenario:

TOBIAS and Ayeisha were married in Texas in 1982. Tobias was a realtor with substantial investments in the Houston real estate market; Ayeisha was a travel agent whose only asset was stock in her brother's computer software business. Tobias began to lose his investments one by one when Houston's economy bottomed out; Ayeisha's stock continued to flourish. When they divorced in 1993, Tobias had no separate assets left, but Ayeisha's separate property investment had grown from $20,000 to $100,000. Legally, Tobias was entitled to half the interest, or $40,000, although neither party's efforts during the marriage contributed to this increase.

It is not uncommon that such a characterization provides an undeserved profit for the non-owner spouse. Some states will allow couples to change the character of community property by contract, some will not. And, referring again to the duty of spousal support, it is possible that a court could order separate property funds to be used to support a spouse upon dissolution of a marriage if community funds have been depleted.

Also, don't forget to consider the impact of any significant debts your potential spouse may bring into the marriage. In most situations, a new spouse is not responsible for premarital debts unless they are assumed in a marital agreement or through a transfer of separate property to a new spouse. However, in community property states, your paycheck automatically becomes joint property with your new spouse. Unless spelled out in a marital contract, a potential for problems exists.

MARITAL DEBTS

Although determination of ownership of assets both before and after a marriage is complicated, owing money to creditors has the potential to create the biggest headaches in a marriage. After you tie the knot, responsibilities in a marriage are divided into joint and separate debt.

- *Joint debts*: Both spouses are responsible for joint debts. Creditors will look first to the marital or community property for these debts, then to the separate, nonmarital property of each partner.

- *Separate debts*: Only one spouse is responsible for separate debts. Creditors will look first to the separate, nonmarital property of the obligated spouse, then to the marital or community property of each partner.

Distinctions between joint and separate debts exist in community property states and separate property states. Many of these areas are not always black and white, so check with a financial adviser if you have concerns about either spouse's obligations.

MARITAL DEBTS IN SEPARATE PROPERTY STATES

Joint debts in a separate property state can include:

- Debts incurred for the necessities of life, such as food, clothing, shelter, and medical expenses
- Debts incurred in the name of both spouses
- Debts incurred based on the credit histories of both spouses
- Debts incurred by one spouse with the permission of the other

Separate debts in a separate property state can include:

- Debts incurred solely by one spouse
- Debt incurred by one spouse to increase the value of separate property that is not a family necessity; for example:

PABLO and Maria live in Florida and have been married for ten years. Pablo receives an inheritance from his father that he uses to buy himself a fishing boat. Maria hates fishing. After a hurricane damages the boat, Pablo takes out a loan to repair it. The loan is his responsibility.

Their next-door neighbors, Chuck and Suzanne, face a different situation. The house they live in, which was Chuck's before their marriage last year, was also damaged by the hurricane. After taking out a loan to repair the house, Suzanne learns that both her share of the marital property and her separate, nonmarital property could be liable for repayment of the loan because the house is a family necessity.

Remember, though, that a creditor may look to jointly owned property to satisfy a separate property debt if a spouse lacks separate property funds to satisfy the obligation. In most cases, the separate property of one spouse is exempt from creditors of the other spouse if the obligation is a separate debt.

MARITAL DEBTS IN COMMUNITY PROPERTY STATES

Joint debts in a community property state include only those debts incurred during the marriage. The only exceptions to this blanket rule would be (1) debt incurred by one spouse to increase the value of separate property (as in Pablo and Maria's example) or (2) debts that do not benefit the community. For example:

REMEMBER Geoffrey's mid-life crisis a few pages back? A month before he files for divorce, Geoffrey takes his girlfriend on a trip to Mexico. He also buys her an expensive "friendship" ring. Although Nicole and Geoffrey are still legally married, the court rules that these obligations must be paid out of his separate property.

Remember, though, that a creditor may look to jointly owned community property to satisfy a separate property debt if a spouse has no separate property funds to satisfy the obligation.

INTERSTATE ISSUES

As if the foregoing explanations were not complicated enough, many couples find themselves in a position where they are forced to deal with the laws of more than one state. If you move from one state to another during your marriage, or if you have a commuter marriage between two states, it is essential that you become informed about the laws of the states that can affect the characterization of your marital property. Different states have different residency requirements before their laws apply, as well as different views on marital property acquired in one state and moved to another.

There is no simple answer to the question of which state's laws control at any given time. The characterization of marital property is also complicated by how it is being viewed: is it a question of how it is owned during the ongoing marriage, or is it a question of how it will be divided in an impending divorce? The actual location of the ceremony has no impact on the applicable laws: the laws of the state (or states) where you live during the marriage or the laws of the state where a divorce is filed have potential jurisdiction over the marital property.

If you move from one state to another, your new home state may have laws that affect the property you acquired in the first state. Also, it is not unusual in our society for couples to own property in many states or even foreign property, which can bring the laws of several states into the equation. In most instances, real estate is controlled by the laws of the state in which it is located. The law that controls portable personal property is not as easily determined. Consider this situation:

ANN and Robert recently moved from New York City to Los Angeles. After consulting with an attorney to determine if they should revise their wills, they learn that property acquired in New York that they considered "his" and "hers" is considered "theirs" under California law. Their attorney tells them that California classifies property brought into the state as "quasi-community" property if it would have been community property if acquired in California. Consequently, the property is treated as if it were community property upon death of one spouse or dissolution of the marriage.

Of course, if one spouse lives in one state and the other resides in another, determining where you actually live may not be so simple. In such a situation, there may be advantages and disadvantages to choosing one or the other state as the marital residence. What works for one individual situation may not work for another; however, the simplest determination of the state of marital residency would be a written agreement between the spouses. Such a situation has overtones of the problems created by "commingling": if the couple can't agree on which state they live in, how will a judge know? Making the decision, as the following couple does, is the wisest choice.

BILL and Sandra are planning to get married next month. Bill lives in Northern California; Sandra lives in southern Oregon. Bill is a psychologist and has an established practice in his city of residence. Sandra is an accountant and also has an established practice. For now, they plan to spend weekends and holidays at Sandra's home while Bill maintains his condo in California. After considering the community property laws of California and the separate property laws of Oregon and discussing the impact of the laws on their personal and professional lives, Bill and Sandra have chosen to execute a premarital agreement establishing Oregon as the state of their marital residence.

Remember the old movies where the wife went to a dude ranch out West to establish residency and get a quickie divorce in a state with lenient divorce laws? Divorce is easier and faster today, but one spouse may move to a new home state and file for a dissolution of the marriage there when the other spouse has never set foot in the state. Obtaining a divorce in another state may be possible after one spouse has established residency there, but the property issues that arise from acquiring property in one state and divorcing in another can be far from simple.

Also, don't neglect to learn how the conflict of laws between separate and community property states can affect estate planning. Chapter 4, Estate and Financial Planning, offers more insight into this topic.

We can alert you to the foregoing issues, but the enormity of the ramifications of the various state laws is outside the realm of this book. Interstate marital issues are an extremely complicated area. Any couple moving from state to state, planning a commuter marriage, or planning to divorce a spouse outside the state of the marital residence is well advised to obtain professional advice.

UNIFORM MARITAL PROPERTY ACT

Looking beyond both separate and community property designations, the proposed Uniform Marital Property Act (UMPA), of the National Conference of Commissioners on Uniform State Laws, is a suggested model for consistency in the laws of the different states. Obviously, the complications of residency and interstate battles over the characterization of property would be greatly eased if all states adopted such an act.

So far, though, only one state has seen fit to adopt this idea. The UMPA creates a new category of property that is neither separate nor community, calling it simply marital property. Wisconsin has adopted a version of this law, which has more similarities to community property than separate property tradition. In this system, property is jointly owned, but management and control is vested in the party holding title.

TITLE TO PROPERTY

As previously mentioned, the importance of the name on the title to property varies from state to state. Examples of assets that come with paperwork attached include not only real estate and automobiles, but stocks and bonds, bank accounts, mutual funds, certificates of deposit, and the like. Although the following information refers specifically to real property, make sure you are aware of the implications of the title on these other assets at the time of acquisition. Question your banker, broker, or attorney until you are satisfied that you understand the potential ramifications of the name on the dotted line.

Acquiring title to property during a marriage can be done in either one name or both. In community property states, even if property acquired after marriage is titled in one name, it is still owned equally (unless purchased with easily traceable separate property funds). In separate property states, the actual title controls, although equitable distribution will come into play upon filing for divorce.

TENANTS IN COMMON AND JOINT TENANTS

Property owned by more than one person is either owned as "tenants in common" or as "joint tenants." The legal distinction affects anyone taking title to property, although some states also have requirements dependent on marital status.

"Joint tenancy with right of survivorship" means that property ownership is shared 50/50. Additionally, if one joint tenant dies, the other can take the deceased's share if right of survivorship requirements are satisfied, even if there is a will leaving the property to someone else. Each joint tenant also retains the right to sell their interest, despite the wishes of the other. This sale, however, would end the joint tenancy and create a tenancy in common with the new owner.

The basic difference between joint tenants and tenants in common is that there is no right of survivorship with the second form of property ownership. Upon the death of one owner, title is left to the beneficiaries in a will or the persons inheriting through the intestate (dying without a will) succession laws established in the state where the property is located. Tenants in common may own property in unequal shares as well, unlike joint tenants. Consider the following example:

BETTY and Frank live in Colorado. Betty is a widow; Frank has been married once before. They plan to buy a house together before their wedding and put the title in both their names. Frank has family money, but Betty has been struggling for ten years to support her two daughters. Although they are in high school and will be leaving for college soon, Betty wants her girls to feel as if the new house is their home, too. Frank has agreed with Betty's decision to buy the house as tenants in common with equal shares as a protection for her children in case anything happened to her. He has also urged her to leave her share of the house to them. Betty and Frank also intend to revise their wills to reflect the estate planning needs of their new relationship.

Couples must determine the advantages and disadvantages of each form of property ownership by the facts of their individual situation. Joint tenancy usually works best for married couples, but if one partner has more to invest than the other or minor children to consider, tenants in common might be more advantageous because the property can then be owned in disproportionate shares.

PITFALLS

A husband and wife purchasing property together after marriage is actually the simplest scenario. However, the issue of title can be particularly sticky for a couple when one party moves

into real estate the other owned before the wedding. Consider
this situation:

S AM and Matty are engaged. Matty owns her own home; Sam
has been renting. They plan to move into Matty's home, but
have several concerns. Sam offered to pay half of Matty's mortgage, but Matty has pointed out that there are many other expenses involved in owning a home, such as taxes, insurance, and
repairs. So, Sam agreed to pay 50 percent of these expenses as
well, but only if Matty deeds him an interest in the property.

  That's fine with Matty, but there's also the question of her equity.
Matty bought her home for $100,000 six years ago. She owes
$91,000 on the first mortgage and has made $32,000 worth of
improvements, $10,000 of which she still owes on a home im-
provement loan. She doesn't see how she can deed 50 percent
of the house to Sam when she has a $31,000 actual stake in the
house and could realize as much as $94,000 from the sale of the
house because the property was recently appraised at $195,000.

Sam and Matty have three options:

1. Sam pays Matty rent

2. Sam pays 50 percent of the house expenses and Matty deeds him
   a proportionate share of the house but retains her interest in her
   initial investment and any potential profit or loss

3. Sam compensates Matty for her current interest in the house and
   assumes 50 percent of the expenses, and she deeds him an equal
   share in the house so that they will jointly share in any future
   appreciation or depreciation

In options 2 and 3, potential tax consequences that might arise
when transferring property from sole ownership to joint ownership before a marriage must also be considered.

  Purchasing a home together before a wedding presents possible problems as well. Check with your realtor or attorney about
any potential pitfalls in this scenario and avoid the following un-
fortunate result:

NANCY and James are both police officers. They lived together in a community property state for four years before their marriage. Two months before the wedding, James bought the house they had been renting since they moved in together. Because he wanted to surprise Nancy, he handled all of the arrangements himself. Five years later, Nancy moved out and told him their marriage was over.

During their nine years together, Nancy paid an equal share of the rent/mortgage and all other housing expenses, including new carpeting and central air conditioning. Legally, however, the house is James's separate property because it was purchased before the wedding and because only his name is on the deed. Nancy is entitled to nothing for the years they lived together before the wedding, although she is entitled to reimbursement for the funds she put into his separate property asset. However, because the housing market in their city is recessed, the house is only worth the amount owed the mortgage lender. James decides to sell the house to get out from under the debt and Nancy can't qualify for a loan on her salary alone to salvage her investment.

Different states have different provisions for taking title to real property and different potential pitfalls. Check with your realtor or attorney regarding the impact of your marital status on any purchase of real estate.

DON'T ROLL THE DICE

Unfortunately, too many couples structure their financial affairs haphazardly and learn the ramifications only in retrospect. Every couple has the right to determine their financial goals by reaching their own agreement. The laws as they exist may not always provide a satisfactory solution to an individual situation. Any couple who is not satisfied with the laws that affect the characterization or the potential division of their marital property should take steps to determine ownership of their assets (and debts) as they see fit, within the boundaries of applicable laws. If a couple does not take responsibility for financial planning, they are gambling with their future.

An "equitable" division of marital assets does not necessarily mean "equal." The fairness of a split is based on each judge's image of the family. Is the man in the black robes an older judge who chivalrously provides ample property for a wife and children? Is he a middle-aged judge who was recently wiped out by a financially devastating divorce and now views all women as money hungry? Or is he a younger judge who believes an able-bodied woman has no excuse to stay home and watch soap operas when she could be earning her keep? Impartiality is a goal that we imperfect humans cannot always achieve. Similar prejudices by attorneys can also impact the financial future of a family.

Reforms concerning the property of spouses are ongoing with the intent to create equality between the husband and wife and to factor in the problems created by the lack of permanence of marriage in our country. Two such reforms include the idea of nationwide laws, adopted by the states, such as the Uniform Marital Property Act previously mentioned and the Uniform Premarital Agreement Act, discussed in detail in a later chapter. The National Conference of Commissioners on Uniform State Laws, the body that has proposed these reforms (along with the Uniform Marriage and Divorce Act mentioned in an earlier chapter), recognizes the complications of fifty different sets of laws and seeks to promote uniformity throughout the country.

After digesting this complicated chapter, such an idea seems a breath of fresh air. Don't let the complications confuse you or intimidate you. If you're interested in more information without the consultation fees of an attorney, head for your county law library. The librarian should be able to direct you to further information regarding the acquisition of marital property in your state.

Chapter 3

TYING THE FISCAL KNOT

Love is blind and marriage is a real eye-opener.
—Unknown

- Reassess life, health, auto, and other insurance to prevent overlapping coverage.

- Review current beneficiaries on insurance policies and company pension plans. Take steps to add your new spouse.

- Consult an accountant to determine the impact your marital status will have upon your federal income tax obligations. Be aware also that the income of a new spouse may have an impact on eligibility of college-age children from a prior marriage for financial aid.

- Notify Social Security of your marriage to ensure eligibility for your spouse's benefits. Also, change your W-4 form with your employer if necessary.

- Remarriage? Consider possible loss of alimony or pension/retirement benefits from a prior marriage.

Unfortunately, money is too often a stumbling block on the path of true love. Even the most compatible relationship is susceptible to the resentments that can flare when two people combine their financial resources. Love/money issues must be confronted on an almost daily basis in an ongoing marriage.

Problems of a financial nature can undermine a relationship. Financial power struggles, whether major or minor, can challenge even the most solid partnership. How do you split expenses, protect separate assets while aspiring to mutual fiscal goals, and build trust in a relationship while coordinating different money styles and habits? A sudden financial crisis or change can also place unwelcome strains on a marriage.

In little more than a generation, traditional male/female roles have changed and the rules have changed with them. No longer does the man bring home the paycheck for the little woman to spend: in most relationships today, there are two paychecks. Because the trend is toward later marriages, both partners are likely to have accumulated more material possessions (or debts) to bring into a marriage. In remarriages, these possessions (or debts) can be substantial, and may include obligations to former spouses or children from a prior marriage.

There is no question that men and women approach money differently. In general, despite the strides women have made toward reaching financial equality in the boardroom, men still have more earning power. With more disposable income, men tend to invest more and take greater risks. Men are also more inclined to measure success by a financial yardstick than women, who place greater value on relationships. In many instances, because making the money takes them longer, women tend to be more conservative investors than men.

Sexual stereotypes are not the only factor that affects how a husband or wife will approach financial issues. Money attitudes are also influenced by family upbringing, age, religion, and the media, as well as each person's own unique financial trials and errors.

Becoming aware of the factors that contribute to your partner's money attitudes can help you reconcile differences in your financial styles. Money too often equates to control in a relationship. No matter how a couple approaches the issue, reconciling money styles is one of the biggest challenges in a marriage. This chapter will present some specific, practical information for the bride and groom with the goal of maximizing joint finances and minimizing losses when two become one.

DOLLARS AND SENSE

Communication and cooperation are the keys to a new couple's successful financial involvement. The couple who can successfully combine love and money have overcome one of marriage's biggest challenges.

The routine business of a new life together begins before the wedding invitations are in the mail. Make a checklist that includes the key points previously mentioned that apply to your relationship. Determining the information you need and the steps you need to take may require consulting your banker, employer, insurance agent, accountant, attorney, or other professional.

Review your financial picture. Are you both satisfied with your knowledge and control of both "your" money and "our" money? Are you both knowledgeable about banking, insurance, investments, and credit cards? A partnership is strengthened when both couples are informed about joint fiscal matters. If you are uncertain about any area, ask for assistance. If you both need more training, sign up for a class or make an appointment with a professional.

When you are satisfied that you have successfully grappled with the everyday issues, turn your attention to preventive financial tasks. Are you prepared to cope with emergencies such as loss of a job or health problems? Prepare contingency plans that fit your lifestyle, such as sufficient health and/or disability insurance and a nestegg of several months' living expenses.

Your goal in tying the fiscal knot is twofold: protect your spousal rights and avoid overlapping coverage (i.e., save money).

Begin your research before the wedding and make sure you follow through.

TO POOL OR NOT TO POOL?

Many modern couples keep their finances separate, whereas others opt to pool all funds. Making the decision on the day-to-day handling of what was formerly "his" and "her" money can be a tough one. The occasional husband may not relish his wife's involvement in family financial affairs; a working woman who becomes a working wife may bemoan her loss of financial independence. And in the event that one spouse is a saver and the other a spender, what's a couple to do?

There are benefits to keeping separate property funds separate and continuing to maintain certain assets in one name only, as we pointed out in the last chapter. A bride with her own credit cards should keep a few in her name.

Keeping other monies separate may create logistical problems, though, along with a diminished sense of common goals for the future. Combining funds gives a couple greater borrowing and investment power as well. Determining a financial plan that works might take months; many couples struggle for years before reaching a balance. Defining and discussing your money styles is the first step, and setting goals is the second. Compromise and renegotiating must be the cornerstones of your joint financial goals.

While contemplating money matters, don't forget to factor in the "marriage penalty tax." The most recent changes to the Internal Revenue Code mean that legal love may be more expensive than ever before.

THE HIDDEN COST OF MARRIAGE

The "marriage penalty tax" is based on yet another outmoded assumption about family life. The Internal Revenue Code is slanted because of the obsolete idea that there is only one wage earner in an American family.

Considering recent changes to the tax laws, a married couple earning $80,000 a year could potentially pay almost 30 percent more in taxes as a couple filing jointly than as two single individuals. William and Mary provide the perfect example.

WILLIAM, a stockbroker, and Mary, a businesswoman, are planning to marry. Each made $40,000 in 1992—William as a salaried employee and Mary from self-employment. William has a home mortgage and itemizes deductions, whereas Mary takes the standard deduction. William deposits $2,000 in an IRA each year, and Mary contributes to a Keogh plan based on her self-employment income.

Prior to filing their respective tax returns for 1992, their situation looked like this:

	William	Mary
1992 income	$40,000	$40,000
Other income and deductions (net)	-0-	-0-
Retirement plan	{2,000}	{5,200}
Deductions	{12,000}	{0}
Standard deduction	{0}	{3,600}
Personal exemption	{2,300}	{2,300}
Taxable income	$23,700	$28,900
Federal income tax	$ 3,855	$ 5,311
Total tax liability	$9,166	

If William and Mary had been married in 1992 and filed a joint tax return, their tax picture would look like this:

	William and Mary
1992 joint income	$80,000
Retirement plan (Keogh only)	{5,200}
Itemized deductions	{12,000}
Standard deduction (no longer available)	{0}
Personal exemptions	{4,600}
Taxable income	$58,200
Federal income tax as a married couple	$11,649

The tax has been computed based on "married filing jointly" rates. William and Mary could file using the "married filing separately" rates, but would likely find that these rates result in more combined tax.

William and Mary's incomes have not changed because of their marriage, but their combined tax liability has increased by $2,483, just because they have chosen to legalize their relationship. This "marriage penalty" is the result of several factors.

First, William cannot deduct his annual IRA contribution because Mary is in a self-employed (Keogh) retirement plan. Second, Mary loses the standard deduction she enjoyed as a single person. Only the greater of itemized deductions or a standard deduction may be claimed on a joint return. The loss of these two deductions increased William and Mary's joint taxable income by $5,600.

Third, the combination of the two incomes on a joint return means that the total earnings are taxed at a higher incremental rate than it would be for two single individuals. Effectively, William and Mary will be paying taxes on more of their income and paying those taxes at a higher rate than before!

Worse, this increase is a permanent one. They will be subject to additional taxes during their entire married lives (assuming this inequity is not corrected by our lawmakers). Also note that social security, self-employment taxes, and state income taxes (where applicable) have not been included in these examples, and will further exacerbate the situation. Even as we write this, Congress is considering raising the rates on individuals earning over $30,000, which would only increase William and Mary's tax liability.

There is one other caveat to this marital tax picture. William and Mary live in a community property state. Consider a scenario in which Mary, as a small business owner, finds that her company is unable to compensate her for several months. She probably would be able to tough out some temporary hard times because she is married. With William continuing to bring in income to support them both, she may not feel as pressured to rectify immediately the temporary loss of "her" money.

At tax time, however, Mary should not be surprised to learn that, because of the flip side of community property laws, she is also legally responsible for one-half of the taxes on William's income. In community property states, there is no "his" and "her" money from earned income. No matter how financially astute a couple thinks they are, this always seems to come as a surprise. Community property is "for richer or poorer": sharing in community property also means that a spouse is responsible for one-half of the debts of the other.

Mary's accountant made her aware of the hidden cost of her marriage to William, but offered one bright spot of advice. Subsequently, William and Mary changed their wedding date from December 31 to January 1. If a couple is married on the last day of December, they are considered by the IRS married, for tax purposes, for the entire year! By postponing the wedding for one day, William and Mary will have saved almost two thousand dollars in taxes. Now, if William can just talk Mary out of spending the extra money on the reception.

William and Mary's situation highlights the need for professional assistance in determining the impact of tax laws on a bride and groom's financial future. Financial advice for couples varies significantly depending on age, economic status, and dependents. Every situation is different, and generalizations are difficult to make. The following are several other issues and examples to consider when determining your need for professional assistance.

DUTY OF SUPPORT

At common law, a man was responsible for providing his wife with necessaries (the definition of which might vary, depending on the economic status of the parties). This obligation arose because the man was given total control over his wife's assets. As long as the couple lived together, the husband could decide the appropriate standard of living.

This rule of common law had obvious equal protection problems when subjected to the Fourteenth Amendment, and the Supreme Court has held that laws regarding marriage must be sex neutral, with the result that each spouse owes a duty of support to the other. In reality, however, the state is reluctant to interfere in the ongoing family's financial arrangements, unless one spouse is not given "adequate support" by the other.

Unfortunately, the definition of "adequate support" is ambiguous, and courts have often ruled that the one who controls the purse strings during the ongoing marriage controls this standard. In some situations, though, it is possible that this duty to support can create unfair hardships. Consider this scenario:

GRACE, a widow, and Morris, a widower, are Floridians who married in 1980 when both were sixty-nine years old. Grace's husband of forty years died in 1970, leaving her a substantial estate that ensured a secure future for her and a generous legacy for their children. Because of these assets, Grace and Morris signed a premarital agreement. That was fine with Morris—he wanted companionship, not money—though he made it clear he had no savings.

In 1993, Grace and Morris are both age eighty-two and still married. Morris suffered a stroke in 1987. Grace's family assumed that federally funded health programs were covering Morris's medical bills, for they knew he had no money or medical insurance. They did not know that Grace's considerable assets made the couple ineligible for such benefits. Grace checked with her attorney: yes, her premarital agreement is valid and yes, she had signed a document at the time acknowledging that the attorney had informed her that such a contract could not obviate the duty to support a spouse.

Grace didn't tell her children: she just paid the bills, and paid the bills, until there was little left of their legacy. By the time her children discovered the situation, it was too late. They have urged Grace to divorce Morris, but she firmly insists that "for better or worse" means just that to her.

The duty to support, unfortunately, cannot be overridden by a contract between the spouses because it is an inherent, inviolable part of the state's marriage contract. Most spouses are not called upon to pay such a high price, but Grace and Morris's story illustrates the potential for financial tragedy and the high price older couples can pay when they obligate themselves to the state's marriage contract without a full understanding of the consequences.

JAY AND DAISY

The duty to support is not the only issue for couples in their retirement years who wish to marry. Often, these couples must balance a new romantic relationship with the realities of a fixed income, a lifetime of accumulated financial issues, and the expec-

tations of children from prior marriages. Take, for example, Jay
and Daisy.

JAY, a widower, and Daisy, who is divorced, are in their sixties
and live in Denver. Jay recently proposed, but when Daisy
broke the news to her accountant son, he explained that she
would lose her late husband's pension upon remarrying, along
with the accompanying health insurance benefits. He also explained that she will lose the social security benefits from her first
husband upon remarriage. Luckily, Daisy was a schoolteacher
and qualifies on her own for social security. Her son then explained that her monthly check combined with Jay's will put them
in a tax bracket subject to taxation on these benefits.

Daisy cannot believe that she will suffer such a financial
cutback in her monthly income upon marriage. She knows that
Jay's financial picture includes a comfortable pension, but he
has explained to her that his wife's last illness depleted all
of his savings. Suffering a financial penalty upon marriage
does not seem fair when they have been contemplating the
comfortable companionship they could enjoy in their later
years.

Jay and Daisy each own a home where they raised their children and where their grandchildren come to visit. When they
marry, they will be faced with the issue of where to live and how
to handle disgruntled children who don't want the family homestead sold. Daisy has a daughter who worries that the family
antiques, many from her father's family, will end up in the
clutches of Jay's family if her mother dies first.

Jay and Daisy made an appointment to see the attorney who
handled Daisy's husband's estate. Daisy explained her daughter's concern about the family antiques. The attorney assured
them that careful planning and the execution of new wills would
ensure that they provided not only for each other, but for other
loved ones.

Jay and Daisy then went to see Jay's accountant to discuss their plans for the future. He told them that one aspect of the marriage they failed to consider was that homeowners age fifty-five or older can exclude from taxation up to $125,000 of gain realized on the sale of their residence. This is a one-time opportunity.

As two single individuals, Jay and Daisy would each have the right to save these taxes on the sale of their homes. But, if they wait until after they marry to sell the houses, they will be entitled to this tax saving on one house only. If one of them sells their home before the marriage, the other would lose this right after the marriage because their new spouse had previously enjoyed this tax savings and could not benefit from it again.

For tax planning purposes, the best thing Jay and Daisy could do is sell both their homes before the wedding. This would be the only way they could shelter the income from both houses. After earning his fee with this information, the accountant explained the impact of marriage on their social security retirement benefits. Both Jay and Daisy currently receive approximately $10,000 per year from social security, and each receives approximately $13,000 per year from pensions and/or investment income. In the past, with a total income of less than $25,000, neither has had to pay taxes on social security benefits.

However, the accountant points out, $25,000 is the base amount a *single* person may receive without incurring a tax liability on social security. A married couple is allowed only $32,000 as a base amount. This means that, because Daisy has qualified on her own for social security benefits, once they marry they can expect to be taxed on a portion of the benefits for the first time. Unfortunately, they also learn that tax exempt income from investments may also be considered when determining this $32,000 figure.

Jay and Daisy, convinced that they now know all of the pitfalls, leave the meeting realizing how burdensome the laws can be for older couples in their situation. They are faced with balancing sentiment and finances when making a decision about their homes.

PAT AND MIKE

Young couples about to marry for the first time usually do not face such complicated financial issues. Take, for example, Pat and Mike:

P AT, age twenty-two, and Mike, age twenty-three, are planning their wedding along with their graduation from college in June. Mike will be taking over his family's business; Pat will be teaching school, although her goal is to become a school counselor. Mike and Pat will start working in September after the wedding and an extended honeymoon. Together, they expect to earn about $12,000 from September to December.

In that federal withholding tables are based on projected annual income, both Pat and Mike need to make sure that the tax withholding from their paychecks is closely aligned with their expected earnings. Too much withholding might mean a nice refund next April, but Pat and Mike need the money now. Allowing Uncle Sam to use this money interest free doesn't make sense for their economic circumstances.

Also, Pat and Mike should give careful consideration to starting a systematic savings program now instead of later. Luckily, Mike has a trusted financial adviser associated with the family business. The adviser has explained to Mike the power of compound interest. The earlier a young couple starts a systematic savings program, the more they will have down the road.

Mike is considering the practical, if not romantic, notion of opening matching IRAs as a wedding gift. Mike knows that the federal tax deduction for annual contributions to an IRA could be affected by other factors in future years, but believes the interest that accumulates each year on a tax deferred basis until withdrawal is an important key to wealth accumulation. Basic financial advice for their early years will start them out on the right foot. As Mike builds the family business, he will rely on more sophisticated financial planning.

YOURS, MINE, AND OURS

Financial conflicts are magnified when there are obligations to former spouses or children, as with Jay and Daisy. The variations of the potential pitfalls are countless.

ISAAC, a lobbyist, and Ebony, a congressional aide, are planning to marry this year in Washington, D.C. Ebony has never been married and has no children, but Isaac has a teenage son from his first marriage who is not happy about his father's upcoming nuptial. Isaac is concerned about his son's emotional adjustment to a new stepmother, but he is also concerned about the potential legal and financial complications a new family will create. Isaac has talked to both his accountant and his attorney about this situation, and has come up with what he feels in a workable solution to their current situation.

Isaac plans to create a "life estate" in the home he owns, and where they will live, for Ebony's benefit. This will mean that she can live in the home as long as she wants if she survives him, but she will have no other legal interest in the property. Upon her death, the "remainder" will pass to Isaac's son, who will have legal title to the home. If Isaac and Ebony do have children together, he will revise his will and make provisions for their child or children. Isaac's solution works well as an estate planning tool for blended families.

BEFORE YOU TIE THE KNOT . . .

Professional financial assistance from your certified public accountant, certified financial planner, or attorney is invaluable when determining how to put your best financial foot forward in a new marriage. Every state has different laws, every couple has unique problems, and the tax laws are constantly changing. A complete understanding of how marriage affects your pocketbook *before* you tie the knot will save you fiscal headaches in the future.

Chapter 4

ESTATE AND FINANCIAL PLANNING

Grow old along with me! The best is yet to be.
                            —Robert Browning

- What are the intestate succession laws in your state?

- Prepare a last will and testament or review your existing will.

- If you have minor children, appoint a trustee and/or guardian for them in your will.

- Learn the everyday steps that will allow your spouse to own marital assets without the delay of probate.

- Learn how estate planning can avoid unnecessary attorneys' fees and minimize taxation of your property.

- Remarriage? Take the proper legal arrangements to avoid unintentionally disinheriting your children and/or avoid conflicts with the new spouse over your estate.

It has been estimated that nearly two-thirds of all adults do not have adequate wills. Over 95 percent have failed to prepare other estate planning instruments such as trusts, powers of attorney, or living wills. You don't have to be rich to be a candidate for estate planning.

In fact, estate planning should be an ongoing activity at every stage of a married couple's life. Any couple old enough to marry is old enough to execute a will, and any couple bringing children into the world without making plans for the distribution of their estate can count on undue hardship for a surviving spouse and heirs.

YOUR ESTATE

As a spouse, your estate consists of both separate property and your share of marital property. Your home, savings, retirement accounts, insurance proceeds, and personal possessions are included. Again, don't forget about debts and obligations as well. Monies owed to creditors and unpaid taxes also figure in your estate.

A court with the proper jurisdiction (often called a probate court) will determine how your assets are owned after your death. If you have a valid will, your property will be distributed according to your wishes. Without a will, the court distributes your estate according to the laws governing "intestate succession."

INTESTATE SUCCESSION

If a person dies without a valid will, they have died intestate. All states make provisions for the distribution of an estate to your family through intestate succession. If you do not tell the state what provisions should be made for your family through a valid will, the state will step in and determine where your property goes based on distribution laws.

As usual, there is no consensus among the states. In community property states, provisions are made for the inheritance of both separate and community property. In most situations, one-half of the community property remains the property of the surviving spouse and only one-half passes through the decedent's estate. Some states, recognizing the trend toward remarriage, make provisions for children from a prior marriage. Other states provide inheritance for parents or siblings if there are no children from a marriage.

Also of interest are the common law theories of *dower* and *curtesy*. Dower is the right of a wife to enjoy a portion of her husband's estate after his death; curtesy is the name given to a husband's similar right. These remnants of common law remain on the books in some states today. Appendix A outlines the laws of intestate succession of the fifty states in detail, but here are a few common results:

IN Colorado, if Jay and Daisy marry and do not execute a will, each would receive one-half of the other's estate upon death. Jay's children from his prior marriage would divide the other one-half of his estate, and Daisy's children from her prior marriage would divide the other one-half of hers.

IN Texas, William and Mary would inherit only one-half of the community estate from the other because one-half would already belong to the surviving spouse. As for separate property (property brought into the marriage or acquired by gift or inheritance during the marriage), each would receive a one-third life estate in the other's separate real property upon the other's death (i.e., the right to use the property during their lifetime), after which it would revert to the decedent's other heirs. They would also receive an outright one-third interest in any separate personal property of the other.

IN Washington, D.C., if Isaac failed to plan ahead and execute that will he was planning, he could leave Ebony in a fix. Upon his death, Ebony would inherit one-third of their home, and Isaac's son would inherit the other two-thirds. Because the son is still a minor, and no provisions were made in a will for a trustee to handle his money, Ebony and an unsympathetic stepson would become bound together by expensive red tape.

IN New Orleans, if Sam and Matty had no minor children and failed to execute a will, they could face in-law squabbles. Each would inherit one-half of the other's estate, with surviving parents taking the other one-half.

LAST WILL AND TESTAMENTS

The right to inherit from a spouse is an important benefit of marriage. As can be seen in the foregoing situations, however, executing a valid will is probably simpler than sorting through your home state's intestate succession laws. If you have children from a prior relationship, executing a will becomes even more important.

A simple will guarantees that you have control over who receives your assets after your death. Attorneys don't make money drawing up wills—they make money probating estates for people who neglect to execute them.

A will is, simply, a document that specifies who receives your property when you die. It's easy to make and gives you the opportunity to leave your property to the people of your choice, not the people designated by statute if you die without one. Also, a will can be easily revoked if you change your mind about any bequests you might have made.

Anyone who has attained adult status in their home state and who is of sound mind can make a will. The differences in state laws make it imperative that you contact an attorney to prepare your will. The statutes vary from state to state, so using a standard form can be dangerous. A simple will, without elaborate bequests, can be prepared for a minimum amount of money. In fact, many attorneys use will preparation as a "loss leader" to attract new business.

Once you have stopped procrastinating and have executed your last will and testament, store your will in a safe place. Putting the will in a safety deposit box is a potential problem, or at least an inconvenience, unless your executors have access to it.

If you have children from a prior relationship, or intend to start a family, do not overlook the important concern of appointing a guardian or trustee for minor children. These issues are discussed in greater detail in chapter 9, Parental Rights and Duties.

CHANGING YOUR WILL

It is not a bad idea to have an existing will reviewed upon a move to a new state. Not only will this verify that the will is still valid but it will also protect a couple from the potential for problems when moving from a separate property state to a community property state or vice versa. Consider this troublesome situation:

IRWIN and Joanne have been married twenty years and have lived all their lives in a separate property state. Irwin is an engineer; Joanne has worked in their home and raised three children. Last year, they retired to a community property state. Irwin was playing golf one day and dropped dead of a heart attack. At the funeral, Joanne learned that Irwin had a son by his former secretary and that his will divided their marital assets, all of which were in Irwin's name, equally among his four children. In their former state, Joanne would have been entitled to, at least, her dower rights in the estate; in the community property jurisdiction, she has no rights to his property.

Conversely, this might be the result in a move from a community property state to a separate property state:

KATE, a teacher, and Maurice, a law enforcement agent, were married five years. Maurice had two young children from a prior marriage. A job opportunity necessitated a move from a community property state to a separate property state. Shortly thereafter, Maurice was killed in the line of duty. Although he executed a will that he believed would take care of his young children, this turns out not to be the case. Kate takes her share of the community property, then exercises her widow's election in one-third of his separate property and his share of the community property, leaving substantially less for his children than Maurice originally planned.

Proper planning can avoid such inequitable results. Also, depending on the laws of your state, your will may need to be changed under the following conditions:

- When you marry
- When you divorce
- When children are born or adopted
- When you accumulate significant property
- When federal legislation might affect your will

In many states, marriage, divorce, or the birth of children might actually nullify all or part of an existing will. If you currently have a will and wish to revoke it, this can be accomplished in the following ways:

- Execution of a new will with revocation language
- Destroying the will itself, preferably in front of witnesses, to eliminate the possibility of testimony that the will is merely missing

HOLOGRAPHIC AND JOINT WILLS

Handwritten (holographic) wills are valid in many states, but are not recommended. They are looked upon with suspicion by the courts, and rightly so. A handwritten will is a risky business; the potential for fraud is obvious.

Joint wills should also be avoided. This type of will attempts to dictate to the survivor how the deceased's property will be

distributed upon the survivor's death. Obviously, once someone
has inherited your property, it will be impossible to enforce what
they do with it. It seems useless to try.

LIVING WILLS

In a landmark July 1990 ruling, the Supreme Court indirectly
supported the concept of a living will when the family of a co-
matose Missouri woman was denied the right to terminate treatment because the woman had not made her wishes known. The
inference made by the court was that a person who had executed
a living will would give her doctor or family the right to refuse
treatment.

The name itself is a misnomer and is confusing to the layman,
who assumes such a document is connected with a Last Will and
Testament. A more appropriate name for such a document is
Directive to Physicians.

A living will gives a person the right to spell out how much
medical care, if any, they want if they become critically or ter-
minally ill and can no longer make their wishes known. Such a
document must be unambiguous. Today, all states recognize a
living will.

TRANSFERRING ASSETS OUTSIDE YOUR WILL

Because of the marital deduction, married couples may have
nontaxable estates worth up to $1.2 million. With a small, non-
taxable estate, probate can be a simple process. However, avoiding state or court involvement in your financial affairs is always
wise. Here are a few simple suggestions to accomplish this goal:

Insurance. The distribution of proceeds from life insurance
policies are not determined by a will (or lack thereof) but by the
named beneficiary (or beneficiaries) on the policy. The insured

can, however, name his estate as the beneficiary and provide
liquidity to pay expenses. Please note that the insurance proceeds are exempt from *income* taxes, but, if the estate is large
enough, may be subject to *inheritance* taxes.

Gifts. Spouses are not required to pay gift taxes on gifts of
property to each other. The Internal Revenue Code permits a
donor to give up to $10,000 each year for any other donee (such
as children) with no gift tax consequences. The $10,000 can be
in money or in property. If in property, it is the market value of
the property on the date of the gift. This is an excellent tool to
reduce one's estate. In that the future earnings and/or appreciation of the gift are also removed from one's estate, this has a
double benefit. The IRS requires that a gift tax return be filed
on gifts exceeding $10,000. It is wise to file a return if property
is given, even if less than $10,000, to remove any future question
about fair market value at the time of the gift.

Pensions or retirement benefits. Again, most pensions and retirement benefits are governed by a contract with the party paying out the funds. However, if a spouse does not take the proper
steps to name a husband or wife as beneficiary, these funds could
be subjected to probate.

Joint tenancy. Discussed at length in the section on home ownership, this method of ownership is also valuable for property
such as bank accounts, mutual funds, certificates of deposit, and
automobiles. Joint tenants share ownership in equal shares and,
with proper language ensuring right of survivorship, own the
property in its entirety upon the death of the other. This form
of ownership can be critical for bank accounts used for everyday
expenses, as funds in the name of the deceased might be inac-
cessible for months. Also, in the event of a spouse dying intestate, a larger share of the property is guaranteed for the
surviving spouse.

Trusts. This form of estate planning is discussed at length in the next section.

LIVING AND TESTAMENTARY TRUSTS

A trust is an important tool in proper estate planning. With it, you can reduce or eliminate income taxes and estate taxes, avoid probate, and protect your heirs. When you give property in trust, you are allowing someone else to manage your property for the benefit of yourself or your beneficiaries.

Trusts are of two basic types: testamentary and living (sometimes called inter vivos). Testamentary trusts are created by your will and take effect after death. A testamentary trust does not have tax advantages, but does allow you to use assets for the benefit of one person during their lifetime, with the remaining principal to be left to another after the beneficiary's death.

Living trusts, as the term implies, are created during your lifetime, but can continue after death. There are two types of living trusts: revocable or irrevocable. The main advantage of a living trust is that it can be used to avoid probate. However, setting up and maintaining the trust can be an expensive proposition. This form of estate planning is recommended only for those couples with significant assets or with real estate holdings in more than one state. The difference between revocable and irrevocable trusts is explained in the following material.

REVOCABLE TRUSTS

A trust is revocable if you, as grantor, can alter or revoke the terms, conditions, or beneficiaries of the trust. There is no income tax benefit to this type of trust, but there are other advantages. The property placed in a revocable trust can be managed by a trustee and the income paid to you during your life. At your death, the principal of the trust is paid to your beneficiaries. The assets of the trust are not subject to probate.

Probated estates are subject to public scrutiny; revocable trusts are not. This allows you to retain privacy over your assets. The assets will, however, be included in your estate for inheritance tax purposes because you retained the right during your life to revoke or alter the terms and beneficiaries of the trust.

IRREVOCABLE TRUSTS

An irrevocable trust is just that: once set up, you cannot revoke it or alter its terms. In this type of trust, you do not pay the tax on the trust income. That burden is passed to the trust itself or to its beneficiaries if the income is distributed. The property placed in the trust is also removed from your estate, although there might be gift tax consequences, depending on the value of the property. If you need to know more about the use of trusts in your estate planning, discuss the subject with your accountant or attorney.

FINANCIAL PLANNING

Financial planning is an ongoing systematic approach to planning for your financial needs in the future. It is a continuous process of maximizing available financial resources. This future time may be retirement, but it also might be education for your children, care of an elderly parent, or protection against some major calamity. As an organized discipline, financial planning has only recently appeared on the scene, but the component parts have long been a part of our financial lives.

In the past forty years, Americans have attained a level of affluence and standard of living never before accomplished. With this status has come problems: inflation; huge levels of personal and governmental debt; the near collapse of the social security system; increasing dependence on imported goods and supplies, with the resultant loss of jobs and capital to foreign markets; and the actual collapse of many banks and savings and loan institutions.

These problems do not have simple solutions, but, as baby boomers look ahead to their retirement years, personal savings programs clearly need to be implemented to make the golden years comfortable. Baby boomers are beginning to feel the triple squeeze; that is, education for their children, support of their parents, and retirement savings for themselves.

Rare indeed is the individual who stays with the same employer for forty years. Most of us change jobs every seven to ten years. It is not likely that an employer-funded retirement plan will meet our retirement needs. We have also programmed ourselves to doubt that we will see any benefit from the thousands of dollars we annually pump into the social security coffers.

Even so, because Americans are not savers, we must rely heavily on company pension plans and social security to provide for our needs after retirement. However, studies tell us repeatedly that this will not be enough. It is estimated that only one out of a hundred retirees is completely self-supporting. The rest depend, to varying degrees, on family, friends, or government.

SET GOALS AND OBJECTIVES

A well-developed financial plan can enable you to realize your financial goals and objectives in a deliberate, organized manner. To help you meet your goals and objectives, the first step is to define carefully what those goals and objectives are.

If you can clearly state your goals, you have accomplished several things. First, you have had to consider exactly what those goals are. Second, you have had to prioritize these goals in some manner. Third, you have probably prioritized achievable goals in considering your present and foreseeable circumstances.

Once you have completed this analysis, you are in position to implement the steps necessary to achieve overall goals. A financial plan that makes sense for you can be developed after a thorough analysis of your currently available resources and the resources you are likely to generate in the future.

A financial planner will want to find out as much as he can about you. It is his or her job to present those options to you that will best help you achieve your objectives. Depending on your current resources and future needs, the planner might present recommendations that make use of various types of insurance or investment programs that can accomplish these objectives.

The designation Certified Financial Planner, or C.F.P., is reserved for those individuals who have completed a prescribed course of study. This course of study was originally administered, and the designation awarded, by the College for Financial Planning in Denver. Since 1985, the designation has been awarded by an independent governing board that recognizes other approved financial planning programs. Candidates must demonstrate their proficiency by passing a series of written exams on such subjects as risk management, investments, taxation, retirement planning, and estate planning.

In addition, a candidate must satisfy certain other criteria, including actual work experience. Once awarded, in order to maintain the designation, the C.F.P. must also meet annual education requirements.

Because of education, experience, and knowledge of their clients' financial affairs, C.P.A.s seem the professional most often looked to for financial planning. In recognition of this, the American Institute of C.P.A.s, in 1987, developed a curriculum of study for those C.P.A.s desiring to add personal financial planning to their practice.

Before you engage someone as your financial planner, inquire about their educational qualifications and experience. You should also find out if their fee is based on the actual number of hours they will spend working on your plan or from commissions earned on investment products they recommend to you.

There is nothing wrong with accepting commissions. Indeed,

such a practice can reduce the direct out-of-pocket cost of a financial plan to you, the consumer. However, it is important to be aware of any commissions the planner may be receiving. With a fee based on hours worked, this is not an issue.

MAINTAINING A VITAL PAPERS FILE

State and federal laws impacting your financial future are complicated and ever changing. A financial expert or attorney can be critical in planning the future. Yet the most basic element of fiscal fitness can be simple organization. Leaving a paper trail is the easiest way to eliminate headaches and protect yourself and your spouse. Set up a simple filing system with your spouse that includes the following records:

- *Contacts:* Names, addresses, and telephone numbers of accountants, attorneys, financial planners, and stockbrokers, and the location of any safe-deposit boxes
- *Banking and investments:* List of accounts, stocks, bonds, mutual funds, and appropriate records
- *Real estate:* Copies of leases, deeds, home-improvement records, and so on (this file is very important if you own both separate and marital real property)
- *Insurance:* Copies of all policies and inventories (include cemetery plots and prepaid burial plans)
- *Pension plans and IRAs:* Documents relating to your retirement benefits
- *Taxes:* Copies of returns and documentation
- *Credit and debt:* A list of monies owed, with account numbers, credit agreements, and names, addresses, and telephone numbers of debtors
- *Automobiles:* Title, liens, and registration and licensing information for every vehicle you own

- *Last will and testaments.* (As previously mentioned, placing a will in a safe-deposit box can create problems unless your heirs have access. Keep the original at home, a copy in your safe-deposit box, and verify that your attorney has a copy as well. A lost will is almost as good as the document itself when the attorney or witnesses are available to testify to its content, so don't worry unduly about losing your original.)

- *Personal:* Birth certificates, marriage licenses, military discharges, and so on

Chapter 5

MARITAL CONTRACTS

Always get married early in the morning. That way, if it doesn't work out, you haven't wasted a whole day. —Mickey Rooney

---

- The state's contract can conflict with financial issues in your relationship.

- A marital contract allows a couple to modify many of the rights and responsibilities of the marital laws of their state to fit their needs.

"Till death do us part" is still the language used in most weddings. Couples enter marriage with the hope of making a lifetime commitment. If this goal is not reached or if a spouse dies, the desire to be a couple is so ingrained that most will marry again.

The inability of the marriage laws to meet the needs of many couples makes the concept of a marital agreement quite positive, despite the bad publicity premarital agreements have received. The freedom to structure a relationship should not be determined by laws that do not reflect the changing realities of family life in America today.

There is no firm tradition of marital contracts in our country because of the inherent resistance to comparing love to a business deal. Many civilized societies through the ages, however, have documented marital agreements with written documents.

Celebrities and the media have made couples aware of the concept of a contract executed between a married couple, whether terming it a premarital, prenuptial, antenuptial, or post-marital agreement. The rich have known about them for years, but middle-class America, alarmed about the rising divorce rate, is eager to know more.

WHO NEEDS THEM?

- Anyone about to enter a marriage who is concerned about the inadequacies of marital laws in the face of today's social realities

- Anyone who is remarrying

- Anyone concerned about protecting the assets of children from a prior marriage

- Anyone who has a financially dependent parent

- Business owners—particularly of professional practices, and particularly those with business partners—because a spouse effectively becomes a silent partner in the business

- Anyone with significant separate property in states where a spouse is entitled to a share of income from separate property

- Anyone whose intended spouse has significant premarital responsibilities, such as alimony, child support, or tax obligations

- Anyone cautious enough to prefer a written record of the ownership of assets to avoid confusion in the future from creditors or other family members

It's not romantic; it's practical. And limiting a spouse's take upon divorce is far from the only purpose, despite the perception gleaned from the popular press. Doesn't it make sense to make decisions under the best of circumstances instead of during the emotional upheaval of a troubled relationship?

As with most things, there's good news and bad news about private marital contracts. The openness needed for such an agreement is good for a relationship; the implication of a lack of trust is bad. A marital contract can avoid expensive and emotionally debilitating divorce trials, but it's expensive to enforce any contract in court. Such an agreement will reduce to writing the agreement for division of property upon divorce, although it can prevent a spouse from obtaining marital rights upon divorce.

WHAT GOES IN ONE?

The three prongs of marital property are yesterday's, today's, and tomorrow's money issues. The following issues are pertinent subject matter for any marital agreement:

- Personal goals of each individual within the marital unit
- Economic goals of the marriage
- Responsibility for income
- Rights to each other's assets
- Distribution of property upon divorce, including the issue of spousal support
- Inheritance rights
- Division of household expenses
- Provisions concerning children
- Provisions concerning household duties and child-rearing responsibilities

PREMARITAL AGREEMENTS

Before 1979, there were few guidelines for potential spouses interested in executing a premarital contract. Because of the significant lack of uniformity of the laws among the states, and because of the greater demand for premarital agreements, the Uniform Premarital Act was created in 1983 by the National Conference of Commissioners on Uniform State Laws. The act has been adopted by Texas, North Carolina, Arkansas, California, Hawaii, Massachusetts, Montana, North Dakota, Oregon, Rhode Island, and Virginia. Colorado has adopted a similar law.

The Act itself provides an example of guidelines to consider when drafting a premarital agreement, including the provision that all premarital agreements must be in writing. It also provides that the sole consideration for a premarital contract is the marriage itself.

When contemplating a marriage contract, the parties must consider—

- The rights and obligations of each in any property whenever and wherever acquired or located
- The disposition of their property on separation, divorce, or death
- The making of a will, trust, or other agreement to carry out the agreement
- Ownership rights in and disposition of the death benefit from an insurance policy
- The choice of law to govern such an agreement
- Any other matter, including personal rights and obligations, which is not in violation of public policy or any criminal law

Only financial matters between husband and wife may be considered. Support of children may not be adversely affected by a premarital agreement.

A premarital contract becomes effective upon marriage, and may be amended or revoked only by another written agreement. It is not enforceable if—

- A party did not execute the agreement voluntarily.

- The agreement was unconscionable when executed because there was not fair and reasonable disclosure of financial affairs.

- The agreement was written with the intention to promote divorce.

ADVANTAGES OF PREMARITAL AGREEMENTS

Love can't be legislated. Both men and women are challenging traditional notions of their roles in the marriage relationship. The idea of a formal contract that is personalized for your own relationship is gaining greater acceptance. Such a contract clarifies what each partner expects of the other. The court system benefits when its involvement in such personal matters as marriage is minimized.

There are four major advantages to a premarital agreement:

1. The agreement can make a marriage an equal partnership, conforming to the realities of our contemporary society.

2. The agreement leads to greater communication and is a guide for future behavior in the relationship.

3. The agreement helps to identify potential problems, leading to, it is hoped, a quick resolution.

4. The agreement can lend a sense of security to the relationship, as both couples know where they stand.

PUBLIC INSTITUTION OR PRIVATE RELATIONSHIP?

America is founded on the theories of individual freedom, privacy, and equal protection under the law. Uniformity may mean stability in a society, but Americans have never been a nation of conformists.

At common law, a contract between a husband and wife was an impossibility. Because of the idea of unity of spouses, it was viewed as forming a contract with yourself. Eventually, with the progress and improvements in the rights of married women, this outmoded idea was discarded.

Marital contracts, though, continued to be restricted in ways uncommon to other contracts. First, the "essential elements" of marriage could not be changed by agreement (see list under Elements of a Marital Contract). This restriction was prompted by concern that society might be forced to support a dependent spouse if the couple agreed they had no duty to support each other. Also, any agreement made in contemplation of divorce was deemed against public policy. There was also the argument that because the husband was entitled by law to both the wife's domestic services and assistance in a family business there was no valid consideration for a contract.

Legislation and judicial trends continue to recognize personal freedoms, indicating that marriage contracts will continue to gain favor. The freedom to contract traditionally afforded all Americans has now been extended to include contracts between married couples. The courts have begun to uphold such agreements as valid legal documents as long as there is no fraud, duress, nondisclosure, or misrepresentation. The Illinois Supreme Court put this position succinctly as early as 1934 when it stated,

Antenuptial agreements are not against public policy but, on the contrary, if freely and intelligently made, are regarded as generally conducive to marital tranquility and the avoidance of disputes concerning property. (192 N. E. 668)

ELEMENTS OF A MARITAL CONTRACT

To guarantee that the courts take a marital contract seriously, the agreement must be negotiated "at arm's length." Simply, one party gives something to the other, expecting something in return, in a situation where there is no fraud, with neither party taking advantage of the other.

These elements become critical in a confidential relationship. To be safe, there must be full and fair disclosure of all relevant information. If these steps aren't followed, charges of fraud, conflict of interest, misrepresentation, or overreaching by a trusted partner can void the agreement.

Hand in hand with full disclosure, the agreement must be entered into voluntarily, without duress or coercion. Any provisions oppressive to one spouse would be automatically suspect to any judge reviewing the contract.

It is easy to see this is not just a matter of who gets what. To avoid any of these potential problems, it is critical that both parties hire their own counsel to prepare and review the document. If only one attorney is involved in the process, the court is likely to uphold any claims of fraud or duress. The validity and enforceability of your agreement depend on these factors.

There are still a few caveats to marital contracts. The "essential elements" previously mentioned include the following:

- The duty to support a spouse: this cannot be limited by contract (see chapter 3 for more information)

- The duty of procreation: courts don't like contracts where couples agree not to have children or sexual relations

- The duty of child support: provisions limiting future support of children are not enforceable

- The duty of service: a contract that provides remuneration for one spouse for any form of services to each other (i.e., housework, and so on) will probably not be upheld—a

spouse owes a partner these services simply as a result of
the marriage contract

Also of concern to anyone contemplating a marital contract is
the input of the family law judge who might be asked to rule on
its validity in the event of a challenge to the document. Family
judges are often given the right to decide if a marital agreement
is "fair and equitable." Family law standards, which allow a substantive review of an agreement instead of the procedural review required by contract law, give the court the right to pass
judgment on the fairness of specific provisions, instead of the
"cast in stone" eye of a judge dealing with any other contract.

It is hoped, however, that the mere existence of such a contract will help prevent the parties from becoming a statistic. In
the worst-case scenario, many of the issues that must be decided
in a divorce have already been negotiated.

Instead of fostering distrust, the preparation of a marital contract allows the parties to begin open, honest communication.
This openness and preventive planning can head off potential
conflicts that might arise in the future between two parties who
are less informed of the "hidden agenda" of the other.

A marital contract will set out the property each party brings
into the marriage. This is particularly important for second marriages, or in situations where there is family wealth. A marital
contract will deal with daily issues of money management and
control during the ongoing relationship. If necessary, a marital
contract will also set out a division of property upon dissolution
of the relationship.

PAT AND MIKE

Pat and Mike face the issues of property ownership because
of his family business. Mike has explained to Pat that the family
attorney is pushing for a premarital agreement that will protect

the business, and he encouraged Pat to seek her own legal counsel.

Pat's attorney helped her work out an area of concern regarding the issue of children. Pat wants to work a few years before starting a family, take a few years off, then return to her career. She and her attorney, in agreement with Mike and his attorney, have worked out a savings program for Pat, and any future children, that will compensate her for any potential devaluation of her earning power due to the time devoted to the family. A copy of their agreement appears in the next chapter.

Because Pat has been so understanding about relinquishing any interest in his family's business, Mike has made plans to buy a house in both their names, making the down payment from his family money.

The attorneys have also explained to Pat and Mike that, because they expect to be married for a lifetime, they should review and at a later date possibly renew any agreement they make now.

POSTMARITAL CONTRACTS

With all the media attention focused on the idea of premarital agreements, the idea of postmarital contracts is often obscured. Marital agreements are not limited solely to agreements executed before a wedding. A husband and wife, no matter how long they have been married, can execute a contract that covers issues that have arisen in an ongoing marriage.

A postmarital contract can be particularly useful in situations where spouses are facing business decisions that create conflicts. Often, partners in business ventures have reason to be concerned about an estranged spouse's potential for unwelcome involvement in a firm's resources. Or, a spouse may worry about risky ventures in business that could compromise joint marital resources. Drawing up a postmarital contract can ease everyone's mind, as in the following situation:

ALBERT, a doctor, and Vicky, a homemaker, live in Georgia. They faced a potential marital crisis when Albert wanted to risk thousands of dollars on a venture capital deal. Vicky's primary concern is the college education of their two high school children, so she lobbied against the investment of their assets in the business deal. To keep peace in the family, Al agreed to transfer half their current marital property into Vicky's and the children's names, while she agreed to forgo any interest in any potential profits in the "can't miss" business deal. When the deal went sour, Vicky was convinced they saved their marriage by negotiating a financial disagreement.

A postmarital agreement is also an opportunity to update a premarital agreement. It is certainly not unusual to have more assets years after the marriage than before the wedding. Ground rules similar to premarital contracts apply to postmarital contracts. There should be no reason why courts will not recognize such an agreement if similar precautions are taken.

NOW THAT I'M CONVINCED . . .

Whether executed before or after a wedding, marital contracts allow a couple the opportunity to determine how property is to be acquired and shared. Such a contract is particularly helpful for a couple who want an equal partnership in their relationship.

In our society today, the marriage contract of the state does not fit the needs of every couple. Doesn't it make sense to reach an understanding before there are problems, while care and concern for one's partner are at their peak? As love decreases, selfishness increases. A private marriage contract, in addition to the state's contract, makes as much sense as, and is as practical as, obtaining life insurance for each other.

So what now? Examples of premarital agreements, and advice on drawing up your own, are included in the next chapter.

Chapter 6

SAMPLE AGREEMENTS

Conrad Hilton was very generous to me in the divorce settlement. He gave me 5,000 Gideon Bibles.
　　　　　　　　　　　　　　—Zsa Zsa Gabor

- Review chapter 2, "Acquiring Property," and the property distribution laws in your state, set out in Appendix A.

- Then, list the assets and debts you bring into your marriage. Beside each item on the list, note any issue or question concerning current or future ownership of the asset or responsibility for the debt. Urge your intended spouse to make a similar list.

WILLIAM AND MARY

William and Mary are the perfect example of a couple entering a second marriage confronted by issues best addressed in a premarital agreement. Mary owns her own business; William has a son from a prior marriage. Both have considerable assets and considerable concerns about the legal and financial assets of their new union. After all, Mary owns her own business and wants to protect that asset. William is concerned about balancing the demands of a new wife with those of a child from a prior marriage.

William and Mary live in Texas, a state that recognizes the community property theory of marital property. Ten years ago, income from separate property in Texas was considered community property, and the characterization of such income could not be changed by agreement. As an example of how our laws adapt, this law was later amended so that income from separate property will remain separate if the parties agree to this in writing.

This amendment to the law is particularly helpful in the situation of a remarriage: William and Mary have decided that the income from their separate property (her business; his rental properties) will remain separate. William has plans to invest in real estate with his brother in the future, using separate funds for this venture. William believes his separate estate, plus this business deal with his brother, will allow him to plan for his son's college and future without detriment to Mary. The following is a contract illustrating the agreement William and Mary have worked out for their future together:

PREMARITAL AGREEMENT
BETWEEN MARY JONES AND WILLIAM SMITH

This Premarital Agreement is made by MARY JONES, Future Wife, and WILLIAM SMITH, Future Husband. We are not now married, but are making this agreement to set out in writing our understanding concerning the marriage we are planning. Our agreement is as follows:

INTENT

We want to minimize conflicts regarding financial matters in our planned marriage. This agreement is executed to prevent such conflicts.

PRIOR MARRIAGES AND CHILDREN

MARY JONES has previously been married, but has no children.

WILLIAM SMITH has previously been married and has the following child: SAMUEL WILLIAM SMITH.

DISCLOSURE

Each of us has provided a fair and reasonable disclosure of our property and financial obligations to the other. Further, each of us has or reasonably could have had adequate knowledge of the property and financial obligations of the other party.

CONFIRMATION OF SEPARATE PROPERTY

Separate Property of Future Husband. All property listed in Schedule A is stipulated and agreed to be the separate property of WILLIAM SMITH.

Separate Property of Future Wife. All property listed in Schedule B is stipulated and agreed to be the separate property of MARY JONES.

EARNINGS AND INCOME

Income or Property derived from Separate Property. All the income or property (whether from personal effort or otherwise) arising from the separate property owned at the date of our marriage by either of us, or that may later be acquired, shall be the separate property of the owner of the separate property that generated that income, increase, property, or revenue.

Earnings. All salary, earnings, and other compensation for personal services or labor received or receivable by either of us, now or in the future, shall be community property.

LIABILITIES

All liabilities and obligations (contingent and absolute) that exist at the date of our marriage shall be enforceable against and discharged from the separate property of the party who incurred the particular liability or obligation and shall not be enforceable against or dischargeable from the property of the other.

FUTURE PROPERTY

Jointly Owned Property. It is our intent that during our marriage, we will from time to time by mutual agreement have the opportunity to acquire jointly owned separate property. Any jointly owned property will be jointly owned by our respective separate estates. Any property that is acquired by either of us during our marriage, regardless of the source of the consideration exchanged for the property, will be owned only as separate property of the party in whose name the title is taken and will be free of any claim of reimbursement on the part of the other. If the evidence of title reflects both our names, that property will be owned by us jointly as tenants in common on behalf of our respective estates.

Credit Purchases. Any property purchased on credit will be the separate property of the party in whose name the title is taken. If there is no evidence of title, the party to whom the credit was extended shall own the property and be solely responsible for paying any purchase-money indebtedness with that party's separate funds. If title to the property is taken in both our names, we shall both be responsible for paying any purchase-money indebtedness with our respective separate funds.

REIMBURSEMENT

Any payment or contributions by one of us to satisfy the debts or otherwise benefit the separate estate of the other shall not give rise to a claim for reimbursement or an interest in any property purchased by those payments unless we otherwise agree in writing. Any right of reimbursement that may arise during our marriage for payments or contributions made to the other's separate estate to the extent any payment is made by one for the benefit of the other shall be presumed to be a gift to the other party's separate estate.

DIVORCE

In the undesired event that our marriage is dissolved by divorce, each party shall receive the following:

(a) all separate property belonging to that party and

(b) one-half of all community assets.

DEATH

If our marriage is dissolved by death, the survivor shall retain his or her separate property and one-half of all community assets plus any property that may be left to the survivor as a result of the death of the other party. Each party waives any homestead rights that party could assert in the other party's separate property. Each party agrees to execute a will reflecting these provisions within thirty (30) days of signing of this document.

GENERAL

No Third-Party Beneficiary. This agreement is for our exclusive benefit and not for the benefit of any third party.

Heirs and Assigns. This agreement is enforceable by our executors, administrators, and heirs and is intended to be binding on our respective estates.

Amendment. We reserve the right to amend or rescind this agreement, but any such amendment or rescission must be in writing and signed by both of us.

Severability. If a part of this agreement is not enforceable, the rest of this agreement will be enforceable.

REPRESENTATION BY ATTORNEYS

Independent Counsel. Each of us was represented by independent counsel in connection with this agreement.

Full Understanding. We both acknowledge that we have carefully read and understand this agreement. We each understand that our marital rights and property may be adversely affected by this agreement.

EXECUTION

This Premarital Agreement is signed and voluntarily executed on the date of the acknowledgments shown below to be effective on the date of our marriage.

ATTORNEYS' CERTIFICATES

I am the attorney for MARY JONES in the above Premarital Agreement. I have consulted with my client about this agreement and explained its terms to her, and my client understood and voluntarily executed the agreement after consulting with me.

I am the attorney for WILLIAM SMITH in the above Premarital Agreement. I have consulted with my client about this agreement and explained its terms to him, and my client understood and voluntarily executed the agreement after consulting with me.

The contract would be properly notarized based on the laws of the state and signed by the parties and their attorneys. Exhibits A and B would list the applicable assets of the parties.

PAT AND MIKE

As seen in the last chapter, Pat and Mike are preparing their own premarital agreement. Although they are young, Mike has a family business to protect and Pat has concerns about raising a family and losing momentum in her career and education. This is the agreement their attorneys have helped them prepare:

PRENUPTIAL AGREEMENT
OF PAT RYAN AND MICHAEL O'BRIEN

PAT RYAN, Future Wife, and MICHAEL O'BRIEN, Future Husband, enter into the following agreement to take effect on the date of their upcoming wedding. RYAN and O'BRIEN intend to conduct the financial affairs of their marriage as set out in the terms of this agreement.

Each clause of this agreement is independent from the others and, should a court refuse to uphold any individual clause, remains valid and in full force and effect.

RYAN and O'BRIEN agree that they have each provided a fair and reasonable disclosure of property and financial obligations to the other.

I. PROPERTY OWNERSHIP

All property listed in Schedule A is stipulated and agreed to be the separate property of MICHAEL O'BRIEN, including but not limited to that certain business known as CALLAHAN'S WHOLESALE. PAT RYAN agrees that she neither owns nor claims any interest in said business, except as set out in the clause III. below.

All property listed in Schedule B is stipulated and agreed to be the separate property of PAT RYAN.

All property listed in Schedule C is stipulated and agreed to be the joint marital property of PAT RYAN and MICHAEL O'BRIEN, including but not limited to that certain residence at 1709 Oak Place in Cityville, Illinois, to be jointly titled in the names of PAT RYAN and MICHAEL O'BRIEN. The fact that this property is purchased prior to the marriage of said parties shall in no way affect the joint title or characterization of this property.

All property, both real and personal, acquired after the marriage shall be considered at all times to be the separate property of the party having title to said property. All property to be acquired in the future which is not titled in the name of either party or both parties which exceeds the amount of $2000.00 at the time of purchase shall require a separate written agreement.

II. EARNINGS AND INCOME

All the income or increase from the separate property owned by either party, either at the date of the marriage or in the future, will be the separate property of the owner of the separate property that generated that income or revenue. All salary, earnings, and other compensation for personal services or labor received or receivable by either party, now or in the future, shall be separate property.

III. CHILDREN

In the desired event that PAT RYAN and MICHAEL O'BRIEN become parents, it is agreed that RYAN shall have the option to interrupt her employment either during pregnancy or after the birth of a child, as she sees fit. O'BRIEN agrees to pay into a savings account the sum of 35% of RYAN's salary as of the date of the interruption of her employment for a period not to exceed two (2) years per child, said account to be in the name of PAT RYAN and any minor child of the marriage. Said funds shall be 100% from the separate property funds of O'BRIEN and said account shall at all times be considered the separate property of RYAN.

In the event that the terms of this clause are not fulfilled, RYAN shall have a claim for any amount due and payable against the separate property of O'BRIEN.

IV. LIABILITIES

All liabilities and obligations in existence at the date of the marriage are enforceable against and discharged from the separate property of the party who incurred the liability or obligation and shall not be enforceable against or dischargeable from the property of the other. Any liabilities of CALLAHAN WHOLESALE, now or in the future, are in no way to be considered the liabilities of RYAN.

V. DIVORCE

In the undesired event that the marriage is dissolved by divorce, each party shall receive the following:
(a) all separate property belonging to that party;
(b) one-half of all assets titled in the name of both RYAN and O'BRIEN.

VI. DEATH

If the marriage is dissolved by death, the survivor shall retain both his or her separate property, the separate property of the deceased and all joint assets, with the exception of any interest which O'BRIEN claims in CALLAHAN'S WHOLESALE. Said interest in CALLAHAN'S WHOLESALE shall remain in the O'BRIEN family and shall be bequeathed to any surviving heir or heirs, including but not limited to children of the marriage of RYAN and O'BRIEN. Each party agrees to execute a will reflecting these provisions within thirty (30) days of signing of this document.

Each party also agrees that they will execute a new will reflecting the inheritance, trusteeship and guardianship of any minor child of the marriage within thirty days of birth. Each party also agrees that 50% of separate property assets of the deceased shall be bequeathed to any minor child or children, including but not limited to CALLAHAN'S WHOLESALE, and said last will and testament shall reflect this desire.

This agreement is for the exclusive benefit of the parties and not for the benefit of any third party. This agreement is enforceable by our executors, administrators, and heirs and is intended to be binding on our respective estates. This agreement may be amended or rescinded, but any such amendment or rescission must be in writing and signed by both parties.

Each party was represented by independent counsel in connection with this agreement, and this Premarital Agreement is signed and executed on the date of the acknowledgments shown below to be effective on the date of marriage of the parties.

[Attorneys' certificates, signatures, and notary acknowledgements would be placed here.]

EXHIBIT A

1. That certain business known as CALLAHAN'S WHOLESALE, including but not limited to, any stocks or pension plans in the name of MICHAEL O'BRIEN.
2. Individual Retirement Account #558992-39555 in the Cityville State Bank in Cityville, Illinois.
3. One (1) 26" Zenith television and one (1) Montgomery Ward VCR.
4. A 1989 Toyota Corolla, Vehicle Identification Number 149285746104LKHS43.
5. One (1) Honda motorcycle.
6. One (1) Sony Videocamera and accessories.

EXHIBIT B

1. Individual Retirement Account #558992-39566 in the Cityville State Bank in Cityville, Illinois.
2. One (1) 19" RCA television and one (1) Sears VCR.

3. A 1984 Ford Escort, Vehicle Identification Number 104LKHS43149285746.
4. One (1) fourposter wooden bed, one (1) matching dresser, one (1) matching secretary and one (1) matching quilt box, formerly owned by maternal grandmother.
5. One (1) ten-speed mountain bike.
6. One (1) Nikon camera and accessories.

EXHIBIT C

1. That certain parcel of land and all improvements commonly known as 1709 Oak Place in Cityville, Illinois.
2. All furniture and furnishings located at 1709 Oakville Place and not specifically enumerated in Exhibit A or B, as of the date of the wedding of the parties, including but not limited to all wedding gifts, regardless of the origin of said gifts.

PREPARING YOUR OWN MARITAL AGREEMENT

After finishing the text, review Appendix A for specific information on the laws in your state. Then, prepare a list of assets and debts, as suggested at the beginning of the chapter, and suggest that your intended spouse also prepare one.

The information needed in this checklist might require research. Finding current market values of real estate, automobiles, mutual funds might take time. However, doing this legwork yourself instead of depending on your accountant or attorney can save a significant amount of money in the preparation of a marital agreement.

The most difficult part comes after you have both completed the checklists. Dealing with the F word (*finances*) may not be the most pleasant aspect of your relationship, but reluctance to discuss these issues now may only lead to complications in the future. Just remind yourself how relieved you both will feel to have discussed the fears and worries that money issues raise. The ability to discuss sensitive subjects in your relationship can only lead to greater intimacy.

After your discussion, a basic framework for your agreement should be evident. Agree, negotiate, and compromise on issues the checklist raises until you are both satisfied with the outcome. Then, consult an attorney to put your agreement into legal language.

FINDING AN ATTORNEY

If you are independently wealthy and have a lawyer on retainer, skip this next part. For the rest of us, making the decision to draw up a premarital agreement may not be the only hard part. Once the decision is made, how is it acted on? What do the bride and groom do now that they've decided a written agreement makes sense for their situation? Find an attorney you can be comfortable with, both personally and pricewise.

Unfortunately, it's a fact of life that attorneys are expensive. Contested cases and court appearances can be exorbitant. However, the charges for basic services (such as preparation of a simple will or a deed to property) are often quite reasonable. The cost of a premarital agreement need not be a budget buster if you know a few basic facts.

Our favorite story about legal fees comes from Richard Alderman, an attorney, author and professor of law at the University of Houston, and television personality known as The People's Lawyer on the local NBC station. Richard called a variety of law firms for quotes on the cost of preparing a simple will for a single man who wanted to leave his estate to his parents. He was quoted prices ranging from $35 to $750. The moral of this story: comparison shopping will teach you more than you want to know about attorneys' fees.

Attorneys' fees can be beyond the means of mere mortals when matters are contested. Preventing such a situation is the reason to prepare a premarital agreement. If you know what you want and what you don't want before you even approach an attorney, the cost should be moderate.

The best way to find an attorney is a referral from people you know. Make sure, however, that these attorneys have expertise in the family law area. An attorney who handled an auto accident case for a friend may know nothing of family law.

If you are unable to obtain a personal recommendation, there are other ways to locate an attorney, such as:

- Lawyer referral services of local and state bar associations
- the *Martindale-Hubble Law Directory* at your library, which lists education, affiliations, areas of expertise, and biographical data of members of the bar throughout the United States
- advertisements

When dealing with a referral service, ask questions about required qualifications before a lawyer is listed as a family law practitioner. Referral services usually require that the attorney charge a minimal fee for consultations. The *Martindale-Hubble Law Directory* can give you basic information, but may not help in narrowing your selection. Advertisements are riskier than the other two alternatives, but interviewing the lawyer about experience in the family law area and asking for references will protect you if you use this method.

Many states have procedures that allow an attorney to become a specialist in a certain area. Legal specialization means that an attorney has met specific requirements and has passed a written test through the State Bar Association. Attorneys who specialize usually have higher hourly rates, so this is not the only criterion to consider when making a decision.

SMALL, MEDIUM, OR LARGE?

A big firm is perfect for big clients with big problems that cover a variety of areas of law. Big firms usually work for business clients. The disadvantages of a big firm are high overhead costs and the very real possibility that you may pay the hourly rate of a partner although a lawyer not long out of law school handles the work on your case.

A medium firm will cost less and often provide more personalized service. However, the small firm or sole practitioner is more likely to concentrate on individuals or small businesses than either the medium or large firm. Most lawyers who specialize in family law tend to be either sole practitioners or in small firms.

Remember, the attorney works for you. Once you have narrowed down your choices, call the office of each and ask if they offer a free consultation. If this is not available, make sure you are aware of the charge for a consultation before going in. If you are being billed hourly for the consultation, be prepared to use your time wisely.

A sole practitioner with experience in family law should be able to prepare a premarital agreement. Don't forget, though, that this is a relatively new area. It is unlikely you will find an attorney who prepares premarital agreements exclusively. If you find, after all this trouble, that the attorney you are interviewing cannot help you, ask to be referred to an attorney with the necessary expertise and experience, much as a family doctor would refer you to a specialist.

NOW THAT YOU'VE FOUND ONE . . .

You need a lawyer who will both listen to you and talk to you—in English, not legalese. Rapport is important, and will be easier to establish if you are open and honest about what you wish to accomplish. While the attorney is interviewing you, conduct your own interview.

Ask the lawyer the following questions. If the answers are open and honest, there may be a match:

- What is your educational background?

- What is your main area of expertise?

- Will you personally handle my case, or will someone else be working on it with you?

- Do you employ paralegals; and if so, will their use reduce the amount of my bill?

- How much and on what basis do you charge, and can you give me an estimate of my final bill?

- Will there be a problem having my telephone calls returned?

- Why should I choose you over the other lawyers that have been recommended?

The biggest complaint about lawyers is that they don't return telephone calls. You want someone who understands that you want your calls to be returned promptly, but you also should be understanding about the realities of an attorney's day. You don't call your doctor and expect him to come to the telephone. An attorney is in court, interviewing clients, dictating and preparing documents, and sometimes it is impossible to handle every telephone call on the same day. When the staff tells you the attorney is in trial, be particularly patient.

Let the attorney know how important it is to you to have your calls returned promptly, and discuss the situation in your initial interview. You want someone who isn't too busy to handle your needs, but you don't want someone who has too much time on their hands. Ask what you can expect, and if there is a particular staff member who can help if you cannot reach the attorney.

Don't forget that two attorneys are required for the preparation of a valid marital agreement. When only one attorney is involved in the preparation, a legal challenge down the road has a much higher chance of prevailing. Involving two lawyers in the process, however, creates the potential for an adversarial situation. Assure your attorney that this is not going to happen, but that you will be responsible for any additional fees involved if unexpected problems arise. Then do everything possible to prevent this.

There are areas in making decisions about a marital agreement that rely on trust, goodwill, and common sense. A couple contemplating a lifetime together should be able to reach an agreement that is fair to both sides, understanding that compromise is necessary in all aspects of life. Let the document be a blueprint for your marriage; not for the possibility of divorce.

When there is no fraud, no duress, and complete financial disclosure before signing the document, a challenge to the contract is probably futile. The majority of premarital agreements do hold up.

WITHOUT A PREMARITAL AGREEMENT

If a marriage founders, the time, money, and emotional agony of litigation are often fruitless investments. Lawsuits and the court system are expensive, time consuming, and often inscrutable to the average person. No one wins in litigated family cases. The pain and anger take their toll and can be even more significant than the financial loss.

There is less financial stress and emotional pain in any agreed settlement because anger and guilt are inevitably bad for a bank account. In an agreed settlement, you can both win. Taking a case to court, you both lose.

Whether or not a marital contract works for you, knowledge of the laws *before* saying your vows can prevent potential problems during a marriage. Certainly there are relationships that do not require changes to a state-imposed contract to be successful. Make sure you have all of the facts before making the decision.

Marriage is full of compromises. Reducing the details of financial arrangements and agreements to writing is highly recommended. Why shouldn't a couple plan their marriage, particularly if nips and tucks to the state-imposed contract make financial sense?

Chapter 7

SPOUSAL RIGHTS

In Hollywood, all marriages are happy. It's trying to live together afterward that causes the problems.
                                                    —Shelley Winters

---

- Does the duty to support raise any issues in your relationship?

- Do you have a commuter marriage between states or will you be moving to a new state after the marriage?

- Have you discussed the issue of last names for the wife and future children with your potential spouse?

Living together after the marriage ceremony can be full of surprises, but the legal and financial obligations of the new status shouldn't be among them. When two become one, the rules change.

Inherent in the marriage contract, but rarely spelled out, is the agreement between husband and wife to form a lifetime, monogamous union that provides companionship, sexual gratification, economic assistance, and procreation and rearing of children. The spiritual and emotional benefits to be derived from this status, although outside the scope of this book, are well known to those who have fashioned a successful relationship.

MARITAL RIGHTS

Along with the duties and obligations, let's not ignore the privileges of the legal marital status. These benefits, a reflection of society's desire to encourage marriage as an institution, include:

- Health insurance provided for spouses through employers
- An interest in pensions and retirement benefits
- Bereavement and sick leave for family members
- Moving expenses or unemployment benefits upon relocation of a spouse
- The right to visit family members in hospitals and authorize their emergency medical treatment
- The right to file joint income taxes
- The right to claim dependency deductions
- The right to an insurable interest (i.e., the ability to take out an insurance policy on the other's life)
- The right to inherit from a spouse who dies without a will
- The right to sue for loss of consortium, wrongful death benefits, or workers' compensation benefits upon injury or death of a spouse
- Travel packages with reduced rates for family members
- Low-cost family rates at health clubs, museums, and other private organizations
- The right of privileged communications

Many of these benefits are available through private organizations and governmental agencies and need little explanation. However, terms such as *insurable interests, consortium, workers' compensation* and *privileged communications* require at least a brief discussion.

INSURABLE INTERESTS

Husbands, wives, and business partners can "cross-insure" each other's lives. The insurance industry recognizes an "insurable interest" acquired by a man and woman upon marriage. Although everyone has the right to name the beneficiary of their insurance proceeds, a husband and wife can actually take out a policy on the other's life. If you are a fan of late-night movies, this privilege might have ominous overtones, but it can be a practical and useful benefit in some situations.

CONSORTIUM

The conjugal rights of the marital relationship are many. A spouse's role may be wage earner, homemaker, companion, and lover. When a third party interferes with the ability of a husband or wife to be any of these things, he deprives the other spouse of the "consortium" of the first. The most common type of interference is the injury or death of a spouse.

At common law, only the husband could sue for loss of consortium when a third party negligently injured the wife. The theory was that the married woman was the property of the husband and that she owed him housekeeping and sexual services. A wife, viewed as a nonperson unable to bring suit in her own name, had no right to her husband's services and therefore did not have legal recourse upon the injury of her husband.

Most states today recognize the right of a wife to sue for a loss of consortium, based on the equal protection clause of the

Fourteenth Amendment. Auto accidents are probably the most common example of a situation in which a spouse would sue a third party for an injury, although any situation in which a spouse is injured would suffice. Upon the "wrongful death" of a spouse, a situation in which a third party causes the death of a husband or wife, the surviving spouse would also have a right to compensation.

WORKERS' COMPENSATION

The objective of workers' compensation programs through the various states is to provide financial support to dependents of injured workers. Although there have been rare instances of unmarried cohabitants receiving benefits, a legal marital status is usually required before any such award will be made. In a situation where there are children in a relationship and no marriage, that piece of paper can make a big difference.

PRIVILEGED COMMUNICATIONS

At common law, two doctrines existed regarding privileged communications between spouses. The first, sometimes described as the "antimarital facts" privilege, disqualifies the adverse testimony of one spouse in an action against the other. The second is the privilege of marital communications, which bars testimony concerning confidential information exchanged between spouses. These two theories from common law are still with us, although the Supreme Court modified the antimarital privilege in 1980 so that a spouse who wishes to testify against the other may do so.

THE IMPACT OF OUTMODED IDEAS

At common law, marriage was the merger of husband and wife into one entity—the idea that husband and wife were "one." The husband had the right of control and the wife had no legal existence outside this unit.

Under the theory of unity of spouses, a married woman lacked control of her own real or personal property. She could not contract in her own name, either with her husband or a third party, and she could not sue or be sued. If she worked, her husband was entitled to her wages, and her husband was entitled to the children if they separated.

The husband's power was so overwhelming that a woman was absolved of any criminal responsibility for a criminal act committed in her husband's presence. He was held responsible, as she was his to control. This domination extended to the physical. A wife had no right to refuse sexual advances, even if force was used. (Although some states have passed laws against marital rape, others still uphold the husband's right to have sex with his wife on his terms.)

These English ideas were adopted in America until the passage of a variety of Married Women's Property Acts in the late 1800s. As laws were passed giving married women more rights, wives began to be allowed to control their own assets. These groundbreaking laws generally granted married women the right to contract, to sue and be sued without joinder of their husband, to manage the property they had before marriage, and to work without their husband's permission and keep the money from their jobs. These laws were eventually followed by all jurisdictions in the United States, although the theory from common law of a single legal identity of a husband and wife created by marriage continues in the following assumptions:

- A woman and any children born to a marriage will bear the husband's name.

- The husband will choose the domicile of the family.
- The social status of the husband determines the social status of the family.

WIFE'S NAME CHANGE

Tradition tells us that a wife takes the name of her new husband on their wedding day. Surprisingly enough, this name change is not governed by statutory law, as many assume. The tradition of English common law still governs this issue.

The common law rule on names was that a person could use any name they chose if such a change was not made to defraud. Because it was the custom in England, a name change was expected upon marriage, although it has never been required by law. Legally, today as in the past, adults are free to use any name they choose, despite marital status.

A married woman is free to keep her own name, hyphenate her name with that of her husband, or change her name entirely. Professional reasons often prompt career women to keep their maiden name or a prior married name; for example:

MICHAEL Smith and Hope Jones were married last month. Hope is a prominent pediatrician who practices in her hometown, a city of approximately 75,000 people. Michael is a writer who has agreed to relocate to her community. Because Hope is well known in the community, she feels it will be less confusing to keep her maiden name and William has agreed with her decision.

It is not unusual for a woman today to change her name completely; for example:

KIMBERLY Sydney Walters married for the first time in college. Her husband's name was Thorveldsen, so she changed her name to Kimberly Sydney Walters Thorveldsen. After her divorce in 1985, Kimberly resumed the use of her maiden name. Now she

is engaged to marry a man named Chimeleski. Kimberly has decided that this identity crisis has gone on long enough. She has
legally changed her name to Kimberly Sydney, the name she intends to use in the future despite her marital status.

The newest trend seems to combine both the liberated man
and the liberated woman. *USA Today* reported recently on the
idea of creating a new name for both husband and wife. Consider
this hypothetical example:

> JOE Watson and Cheryl Newhouse are planning on getting mar-
> ried next month and plan to have children as soon as possible.
> Cheryl considered keeping her name; she considered hyphenat-
> ing her name; she considered changing her name to Watson. She
> was not satisfied with any of these solutions for herself or their
> future children. Joe then decided that the most equitable solution
> would be for their new family to assume a new name. They have
> agreed on Newson, a combination of both their last names.

A name change, at any time, does not require a court order or
a marriage license to be legal. However, obtaining a driver's license, passport, or other important document is much easier in
our bureaucratic society with the proper paperwork.

Although most women continue to take their husband's name
upon marriage, the issue of what last name a woman chooses can
become a major issue if she marries more than once, or upon
divorce, particularly if she has children. It is not unusual for
courts to refuse to grant a name change to a mother after a
divorce. This refusal is based on the theory that the confusion
created when a mother and her children have different last
names is not in the best interest of the children. Courts in California and New Jersey have previously refused to restore the
maiden name to the mother of minor children, although both decisions were overruled at the appellate level.

Also, interestingly enough, courts can prohibit a woman from
continuing to use her former husband's last name if he requests

that she change it, no matter what her preference might be. Such situations highlight potential controversy that might arise over the name change. As usual, different states have different positions, making generalizations difficult. Any woman who feels strongly about being coerced by the state to take a name she is not comfortable with should consider appropriate legal action.

CHILDREN'S NAMES

Just as tradition dictates that the wife take the husband's name, it has also been the custom that children take their father's name. This custom has served society in two ways: as an indication of legitimacy as well as an illustration of the father's dominance of the family line.

It is not uncommon today for a child to be given a hyphenated name consisting of both parents' surnames. Some couples have come up with the novel idea of having the boys carry on the father's name, whereas the girls take the mother's. Neither choice has made the bureaucrats in charge of such matters particularly happy.

After divorce, parents may disagree about the children's names as well. At common law, the rule has always been that the father's name was carried by his progeny, and this rule continues to be respected by the courts. Mothers may marry again and change their names, but the children retain the father's name (unless adopted by a new spouse).

In most situations, a name change after birth for any child will require the consent of both parents, making the matter more complicated than changing the name of an adult. The rule applied to such a change will always be the "best interest of the child," not necessarily the parental wishes. Factors to be considered when determining the best interest of a child include:

- The name of the custodial parent
- Names of other children in the family

- Any social problems a child might encounter because of a certain name

- The benefit of maintaining a relationship to the parent who does not have custody

The two most common instances of name changes for children through the courts are a child born outside wedlock who later takes his father's name or a mother who wants the child to carry a name other than the biological father's.

Take, for example, a 1980 case decided by a California court. A couple separated after a brief marriage, with the wife pregnant. She gave her daughter, born before the divorce proceedings, her last name. Her husband protested and the trial court and the appeal court ruled that he had a "protectible interest" and a "primary right" to have the child bear his name, although his daughter had never lived with him. On appeal, the California Supreme Court held that the daughter could bear the mother's name, basing their decision on the "child's best interest."

DOMICILE

Again, tradition has dictated that the wife lives where her husband does or that she will be the one to make a move upon marriage. Common law dictated that the husband, as head of the household, had the right to choose where the family lived and that the wife was obligated to follow him and adapt to whatever living arrangements he chose.

This may seem a relatively innocuous tradition, but the rules concerning domicile have often served to exclude wives from benefits based on residency. For example, a woman might be paying low rates for tuition at a state university. If she marries a man from another state, she could lose that right if his legal domicile is elsewhere. In her home state, a new wife might be subject to

higher taxes based on her husband's residency, and might find
that she is no longer allowed to—

- Vote or run for office
- Serve on juries
- Sue for divorce
- Register a car
- Receive welfare assistance
- Have an estate administered

A few states have seen the discrimination behind such laws
and have moved to declare that the residence of a person may
not be abridged because of sex or marital status.

There have also been cases in the past where women have
refused to follow their husband to a new location. Such refusal
has been held to be constructive desertion in divorce cases.
Courts in such cases have justified this action because it "flies in
the face of everything sacred that decrees that the husband must
choose the domicile and the wife must conform thereto," according to one not-so-liberal jurist.

The tradition of requiring the wife to adopt her husband's
domicile has become out of date for several reasons. The justification for the tradition had been that the husband was the only
breadwinner and that the law imposed on him alone the burden
of supporting the family. Today, it is not only the husband's career that must be considered. Rarely is the husband the only
working spouse in the family. Also, because commuter marriages
are becoming common, a couple may maintain two or more residences in different states.

Again, it is hoped that the trend is away from the archaic ideas
that govern the choice of domicile of a husband and wife. Recent
cases have upheld legitimate business and financial reasons for
a wife to refuse to follow her husband to another location, and
it is likely this trend will continue.

Although there are lingering effects of traditional law in many of the marital obligations previously mentioned, the idea that the husband and wife merge into a single entity upon marriage does not have to mean that the merger subordinates the wife's identity. Recent legal decisions tend to favor the partnership concept of marriage—a concept that allows both wife and husband equal rights and privileges under the law.

Chapter 8

A WORD TO THE WIVES

Most marriages are made in heaven. But then, so are thunder and lightning. —Unknown

---

- Statistics indicate that one-half of all marriages will end in divorce.

- Statistics indicate that nine out of ten women will become widows, whereas only one out of six men will become widowers.

- Protect yourself financially with active involvement in all aspects of your marriage's money management.

No-fault divorce has redefined marriage. Today, the good news is that the law recognizes a married woman as an individual with the same rights and responsibilities as a man. The bad news, however, is that this hard-won independence will not serve a wife unless she takes precautions against the social realities of this new role.

EQUAL PROTECTION?

Women have been freed from archaic ideas about their roles as helpmate to the male of the species. They have also been freed from the security of the traditional family structure. Our mothers and grandmothers could devote themselves to hearth and home while the husband played the role of breadwinner, but the law no longer compensates women for dedication to husband and children. Pat and Mike have a friend whose recent marital problems illustrate how tragic the end of a marriage can be.

CATHY and Tom married in college. Their first child was born about the same time Cathy received her degree in social work. Five years later, the couple has three children and Cathy has never found the time to pursue a career. Tom, on the other hand, is an accountant who recently graduated from law school. He also has a girlfriend who is pregnant. Tom, torn between his obligations, has confessed all to Cathy.

Tom is currently working as a self-employed accountant out of the apartment he shares with Cathy and the three kids. He has been unable to find a job as a lawyer in these tough economic times. He handles all of the family finances. Cathy doesn't know much about their financial affairs, but does know there isn't much left after paying for Tom's legal education. She has no job, no experience, no money to pay for day care, as well as a very real concern about the effect the new child has on the rights of her children. Tom has told her he doesn't know what he is going to do, but he wants to have every Thursday night free to visit his girlfriend until the baby is born so that he can "support" her.

A lawyer or a judge cannot come to Cathy's rescue and make it better. Life isn't fair, and often there is no legal remedy for the inequities of divorce or the reality of staying in a failed marriage to feed your children. The courts cannot force a man or a woman to be a good spouse or a responsible parent.

This is the Catch-22 of equal rights for women. Equal legal and financial rights have been hard won, but childbearing and child rearing are areas in which equality cannot be legislated. A woman may find herself in a position where she is expected to be equal to a man under the law, even if she has run the home and raised the children.

Sacrificing a career and earning potential to take care of a family is an admirable pursuit, but it doesn't pay the bills if a marriage fails. A woman without earning potential doesn't elicit much sympathy in the courts today: if she's able-bodied, why doesn't she have a job?

This is not to say that the old system was the answer. What women must learn is how to work within the existing system, and have the savvy to adjust to the new ways of the world.

DIVORCE REDEFINES MARRIAGE

Women must understand the impact divorce laws have on the structure of an ongoing marriage. Wives and mothers understand the importance of life or home insurance for a young family. In today's society, it is even more important to have protection against the end of a marriage, an event statistically more likely than early death, fire, flood, or famine.

No-fault divorce was originally envisioned as a way to eliminate acrimony and to promote equality in divorce cases. Unfortunately, it has resulted in the elimination of the leverage that economically dependent wives once had. Hardest hit under the new rules are older women without outside careers and women in their child-rearing years who have chosen the "mommy track."

The "equality" women have found under the divorce laws has meant that a divorced woman has an equal right to go out and get a job just like her husband, although she may have no training, no up-to-date job skills, and can't find a job that pays more than her day care expenses. A middle-aged woman finds herself competing for jobs with a work force that is younger, better educated, and better trained. It is no surprise that the statistics show that many women supporting children suffer a dramatic decrease in the standard of living they previously enjoyed.

By ignoring the economic inequalities that were already in existence, the new laws did not consider that women who had chosen child rearing were not on an equal footing with men who had chosen careers. Often, the greatest asset of a marriage is the "income stream" from the employment of the spouses. Rarely is career potential of the employed spouse factored into divorce settlements.

As the divorce courts struggle to find fair results in an unfair world, how do they handle the inequity of one spouse putting the other through school, only to be denied the economic benefits of employment because of that education? This is a hotly contested area, and only a few states have begun to follow a trend of factoring college degrees and professional licenses into a division of marital property. It is hoped that more states will follow this trend. Let's hope Cathy's situation proves to be one in which she and her children are protected and compensated in this fashion.

INSURANCE

What can a wife and mother do to protect herself? Any married woman today, and particularly any married woman with children, should consider the following steps:

- She should put title to a portion of the marital property in her name if she lives in a separate property state. She should protect separate property assets from commingling with community property in a community property state.

- She should obtain or keep credit cards and a bank account in her own name.

- She should take an active role in handling family finances. In the event of the disability or death of her husband, she can take over the family's financial affairs. In the event of divorce, the expense of discovering assets is eliminated and the possibility of assets being hidden or destroyed is greatly lessened.

- She should take precautions to protect her ability to be financially independent and self-supporting.
- She should consider a premarital or postmarital contract.
- She should make certain that a valid last will and testament with guardianship/trustee language for all minor children is executed and kept current.

If you are married and there is trouble in your marriage, you should add the following suggestions to the previous list:

- Evaluate your job marketability and take steps to improve it, if necessary.
- Investigate child care options.
- Consult an attorney.

Before the Equal Credit Opportunity Act, it was traditional that a woman relinquished her personal credit when she got married. Today, a creditor is not allowed to ask about a person's marital status on an individual credit application, unless relying on a spouse's income to support the application.

For all women, credit in their own name is a must. Too many women, upon divorce, have found themselves stripped of a privilege they took for granted. Credit is too important a commodity in our society not to be protected. Credit that is easily obtainable with two incomes or on the basis of a husband's salary may be difficult for a woman to obtain on her own at a later date.

Taking any of the foregoing precautions is no more pessimistic than executing a will or buying life insurance. Everyone understands the importance of these traditional protections, but few understand that the drastic changes of the past few decades have created a new set of rules for marriage. Maintaining control of your future, and the future of your children, is your responsibility, and no divorce court, judge, or attorney can do it for you.

Women, whether they work outside the home or not, need to know all of the details of the family's financial affairs. In today's complicated financial climate, a man must appreciate the input rather than feel threatened by his wife's need to be an equal partner in money matters.

A wife needs to be involved in the financial affairs of the family not only to protect herself but to protect her children. The disability or death of a spouse is potentially more devastating than divorce, but one of the biggest expenses of any of these events is the evaluation of family assets. A woman gains not only a sense of accomplishment from an active role in managing money, but protects herself and the ones she cares about. Preparing and maintaining a filing system, as suggested in chapter 4, is an excellent way to stay up-to-date on the family's financial picture.

Money often equates to control in a relationship. Equal partnership in title to assets is also important. If a man insists on controlling the finances during the relationship, it is likely he isn't suddenly going to become generous if the marriage ends. Title to property and maintaining credit as a person, not as a wife, can be invaluable.

A wife often puts education or a career on hold to have children. If her marriage ends, this decision can backfire. To compensate a mother for any school or career plans that are put on the back burner, a couple should set up a savings account to pay tuition at a later date or counterbalance her lower earning power when she reenters the work force.

In the past, marriage for a woman meant a change from control by her parents to domination by her husband. No matter how much property she brought into the marriage, her husband had the right to manage it. Marriage was necessary so that a woman did not become an outsider in society—an old maid, or spinster.

The decision to marry today is usually made for much more

romantic reasons. Balancing the emotional and financial issues of modern marriage, however, creates a dichotomy that is difficult to solve. Love and the law are a complicated combination. Practical considerations should not be compromised because love is blind.

Chapter 9

PARENTAL RIGHTS AND DUTIES

First comes love, then comes marriage, then comes [insert applicable name] *pushing a baby carriage.*
—Traditional

- A woman's reproductive rights are not altered by marriage.

- Parenthood is determined by both biology and adoption.

- The legal duties of parenthood include the support, care, and education of minor children.

- Protect your children's rights with a valid last will and testament.

No one has yet devised a pre-parental contract, even though the adventure of raising children has spawned multitudinous volumes of advice. We will just add a few brief remarks to that body of work and touch on the legal issues of parenthood.

REPRODUCTIVE ISSUES

In ancient civilizations, society often enforced a duty to reproduce on its married citizens in an attempt to assure cultural survival. Today, annulments are granted because of impotency, laws remain on the books prohibiting premarital and extramarital sex so that children are born within the framework of a legal marriage, and marriage between same-sex couples is not allowed because these unions cannot produce children. Having children has always been considered an integral part of marriage.

During the ongoing marriage, the law says that parents share joint responsibility and equal rights in child-rearing duties. But these equal duties only take effect once the child is born. The Supreme Court has overruled a state statute allowing a husband to veto his wife's abortion. Today, it is a woman's decision whether to have children or not. Women do not need a spouse's consent to use birth control and they also have the right to choose an abortion without a husband's consent in the first three months of a pregnancy.

CHILDREN OUTSIDE WEDLOCK

Under English common law, an illegitimate child had no legal rights. Such a child was a *filius nullius*, a child of no one, neither father nor mother. A child suffered both legal and social penalties if his parents did not marry.

Contemporary laws make no distinction between legitimate and illegitimate children. This liberal legal stance comes in handy in situations where the child comes first and the marriage second (if at all). The legal status of marriage, however, creates many benefits for children and remains the easiest way for a father to form a legal relationship with his child (maternity being pretty much a certainty). Unless the parents of a child marry, the father often has no legal relationship with his child other than through a paternity suit or voluntary legitimation proceeding in the courts. The rights of the parental relationship are similar to the rights of the marital relationship discussed in the last chapter, including the right to inheritance and to sue for wrongful death. When a man and woman who have a child outside wedlock do marry, the child is automatically entitled to the legal rights and duties as if the marriage had taken place before his or her birth.

PARENTAL OBLIGATIONS

The parent-child relationship, much as the marital relationship, is a legal status. Although parents have wide latitude in how they raise their child, the legal system has the right to intervene when certain duties or obligations are not met. Parental duties include the following:

Duty of support. All states require that parents support a child. During the ongoing marriage, the duty is an equal one and the division of the responsibility is superseded only by a direct court order. The obligation continues after divorce and is enforced by both civil and criminal laws, as any parent who has faced a jail sentence for nonpayment of child support can tell you. The sex of the parent doesn't matter—both mothers and fathers have served time for shirking this duty.

Duty of care. A parent also owes a child a duty of care, as evidence by the laws against child abuse and neglect. Interference with the ongoing parent-child relationship is not taken lightly, but governmental agencies will intervene if there are sufficient grounds. Punishment is less the issue in these cases than help for the child.

Duty to educate. Parents are also under a duty to educate a child. Each state handles this situation differently, but none looks favorably on a parent who can't get their child to attend school regularly.

Also, a parent should consider the potential responsibility for the acts of their child, ranging from windows broken by baseballs to such serious situations as a minor discharging a gun kept in

the home. The law distinguishes between "negligent" and "will-
ful" acts, so most parents shouldn't sweat "kids will be kids"
incidents (even though good manners may mean making financial
reimbursement). However, when the behavior of a child borders
on delinquent, parents should consult an attorney for the boundaries of responsibility in their state.

INHERITANCE

Inheritance is one of the most important legal rights a child
derives from its parents. One of the first things a parent should
consider after a child's birth is the issue of inheritance, as well
as the collateral issues of trusteeship and guardianship.

The parents of a child are its best caretakers. However, in the
event something happened to both parents, a will sets out a
guardian to be in charge of the "person" of the child and a trustee
to be in charge of the "estate" of the child. Unfortunately, few
parents of small children have wills or have made provisions for
their child in the event of a tragedy. And tragedies do happen.
Consider the following scenario:

GLORIA is a sixteen-year-old child whose mother came from
Mexico to the United States as a young girl. Her mother
briefly married a young man from a wealthy family, although parental pressure on him eventually forced the young couple to divorce. When Gloria was two, her mother remarried an older man
named Manuel, also a native of Mexico. Manuel is the only father
Gloria has ever known. She was planning to go to college until
her mother recently died after a two-year illness.

Gloria's mother left no will and no provisions for Gloria's future.
Gloria's natural father picked her up after the funeral and moved
her into his home in another city. She feels she is treated as a
servant because his new wife requires her to clean the house and
baby-sit for their two young sons. Gloria wanted to stay in her own
home, in her own high school, and with Manuel, but her stepfather
has no legal relationship with Gloria. Her biological father does

and is entirely within his rights to move Gloria into his house. The young girl has lost not only her mother, but her entire life as she knew it. Eventually, she runs away from her father's home, drops out of school, and becomes pregnant herself.

Unfortunately, this "hypothetical" situation is actually a true story. This is an extreme example, yes, but serious business requires a serious example. If you have minor children and have made no provisions for their future, take steps to protect them now.

In this day of blended families, Gloria's story raises a second issue: what should her mother have done to create a legal relationship between Gloria and Manuel? If a biological father outside marriage has no legal rights, where does a stepparent stand?

STEPPARENT ADOPTION

Adoption is a legal proceeding where one person assumes parental responsibility for the biological child of another. In most situations, the parental rights of one biological parent must be "terminated" before a new parental role can be established.

Adoption carries with it all the legal duties outlined previously, including the most important of them all—the duty to support. Without adoption, a child whose parent remarries has no legal relationship of any kind with the new spouse or with other members of the new spouse's family. Adoption is the only way to create such a relationship.

However, a hasty decision by a stepparent to adopt can create years of financial ramifications, as evidenced by this story:

GREG fell in love with Linda at first sight. Even though he was just recovering from a broken marriage, she was everything he had ever wanted. Not only was she good-looking, but she was a great cook and she loved football. True, she did have a ten-year-old daughter, but Laura was quiet and sweet. Besides, Greg told himself, he was on the far side of thirty and a ready-made family had a certain appeal. So, after three months, he and Linda were married.

From the minute the ink was dry on the marriage license, Linda began to talk about what a great father Greg was. Laura began to call him "Daddy." Linda would lie beside him at night and cry because her little girl's father never called or sent gifts and it was so hard on a little girl not to have a father.

Two months after the wedding, Linda and Laura stood beside Greg in front of a judge who granted the adoption. Linda sent the papers to Laura's natural father by overnight express and had them back within twenty-four hours. And, though it really couldn't have happened that quickly, overnight Linda didn't feel like cooking anymore and only wanted to eat out. She began to nag that Greg spent too much time watching football. Then she quit her job and told Greg they would just have to manage on his salary. In the divorce decree, Greg was ordered to pay $400 a month child support until Laura reaches the age of eighteen. That figure is approximately 23 percent of his take-home pay, approximately $40,000 over the next eight years.

Again, this "hypothetical" situation is a true story. Adoption is serious legal business: it's probably a bigger step than marriage. You can divorce that nagging spouse, but you can't divorce a child.

This is not to say that a stepparent shouldn't adopt a child. Often, adoption may be the best solution for all concerned, as in Gloria's situation. A stepparent may be a better parent than a biological parent, though they are not, legally, a parent at all.

The biggest obstacle to adoption is the termination of parental rights. Often, the noncustodial parent is adamantly opposed. Unless that parent has abandoned the child and the court rules to terminate the rights through its own power, adoption is not possible.

However, assuming consent is no problem, stepparent adoptions are a simple proceeding. An application seeking the adoption is filed, at which time a social worker will be appointed by the court to investigate the circumstances of the adoption. Most states require that the person seeking the adoption and the child in question have lived together for a minimum amount of time before proceeding to this step.

After investigating the home and the background of the two parents, and speaking with the child if possible, the social agency reports its recommendation to the court. In most situations, the termination of one parent's rights is the biggest hurdle in this process.

Two collateral issues worthy of mention are the right of inheritance from the "terminated" parent and the rights of the biological grandparents of the adopted child. These two factors must also be considered in this decision.

It is possible that state law or the adoption papers can retain the right of inheritance for the child, as it is hoped the adoption process is a benefit to the child, not a detriment. Also, states are beginning to be attuned to the rights of grandparents. If these are issues in a stepparent adoption, consult an attorney in your state to determine current laws.

"BEST INTEREST OF THE CHILD"

Unfortunately, it is often true that the most complicated legal issues concerning children in a marriage arise once the marriage is over. The traditional marriage contract called for the husband to support and the wife to nurture the children of their union. Interestingly enough, at common law, the father was considered the natural guardian of a legitimate child. The father was thought to have a "natural right" to the custody of the children: they were his "property" and his to do with as he saw fit.

This preference for the father as the custodial parent ended with the Industrial Revolution. Fathers left the home to work in factories, and mothers were left behind on a full-time basis with the children. With her growing responsibility came the view that she was entitled to their custody. Today, because so many mothers work outside the home, our assumptions about child rearing are slowly changing again. More and more fathers seek custody after a divorce and, although it is still an uphill battle for most, a man raising a child alone is not uncommon.

The "child's best interest" is always the test for custody. However, the precedent remains that the best interest of the child is served by remaining with the mother after dissolution of a marriage. Despite the equal protection laws, this remains the theme of most judicial decisions on custody.

Chapter 10

MODERN MARRIAGE

Marriage is a lot like the Army. Everyone complains, but you'd be surprised at the large number that reenlist. —James Garner

---

- Congratulations! You've successfully completed the course of study.

- Now, take the written test in Appendix B. When you have completed the answers and followed through with each step, you're ready to apply for that marriage license.

The 1992 Presidential campaign focused extensively on "family values." Just what defines a family in America today? According to a report from the Population Reference Bureau in Washington, D.C., stereotyping the American family can be difficult because—

- Only one in five families consists of a wage-earner husband, homemaker wife, and at least two children
- 40 percent of married mothers work outside the home
- 42 percent of all married couples have no children

- One in five families includes a stepchild
- 10 percent of all families with children are headed by single women

Other statistics show that marriage rates are down and that divorce continues to plague the American family.

MARRIAGE STATISTICS

The National Center for Health Statistics (NCHS) reported in 1988 that the nation's overall marriage rate dropped to 9.7 marriages per 1,000 Americans, the fourth straight annual decline and the lowest rate for marriage since 1967.

CONTRIBUTING FACTORS

In August of 1991, Texas A&M sociologist Dr. Mark Fossett, in conjunction with Dr. K. Jill Kiecolt, a sociologist at Arizona State University, released findings from a study that determined that three factors have helped lead to a decline in marriage rates. They found these factors to be:

- The continued economic self-sufficiency of women, who are less likely to remain in a marriage simply for economic reasons
- The declining number of eligible men in the labor force in comparison to the number of eligible women
- The increased availability of welfare for low-income women, an often viable economic alternative to marriage

LIVING TOGETHER

Another study by the NCHS showed an increased tendency for couples to live together outside marriage. One-third of women ages fifteen to forty-four surveyed in 1988 admitted living with a man outside marriage at some point in their lives. For women between ages twenty-five and twenty-nine, the percentage rose to 45 percent.

CAN MARRIAGE SURVIVE?

These figures do not mean that Americans have given up on marriage. The NCHS reported 2.4 million weddings in 1988, although this total does not reflect just first marriages. A breakdown of the statistics hints at the number of remarriages in this tally.

Of the 2.4 million weddings in 1988, 10.7 percent were celebrated by divorced men marrying never-married women. The big surprise from the statistics, however, was that 10.9 percent of the marriages were between a bride with at least one divorce in her past and a groom who had never walked down the aisle. With many older men marrying younger women, younger men are turning to women who are slightly older—and previously divorced.

DIVORCE STATISTICS

In our modern society, there has been a frustrating lack of permanence in our relationships. Estimates suggest that approximately one of every two marriages ends in divorce, with the average length of a marriage before divorce only five years. Seemingly, the concept of permanence has almost been eliminated from the definition of marriage. How have we come so far from the ideal of a lifetime union for husband and wife?

ORIGINS OF DIVORCE

In England, the traditional religious ruling was that the sacrament of marriage could not be dissolved by civil law: "What God has joined, let no man put asunder." Despite separation of church and state in America, the view of marriage as a lifelong bond, "till death do us part," has been a consequence of religious influence.

It was not until after the seventeenth century that occasional divorces were allowed by special act of Parliament in England. The exorbitant expense, however, meant that this remedy was out of reach for all but the very wealthy. The Church did allow divorce "a meansa et thoro," Latin for a separation from bed and board, in actuality only a legal separation, as the couples remained married in the eyes of the Church.

In 1857, the modern concept of divorce (i.e., a dissolution of the marriage where both partners were allowed to remarry during the lifetime of a former spouse) began in England. The courts of the Church in that year transferred their power to the civil courts.

The United States has always been heavily influenced by the traditions of England. As early as the mid-nineteenth century, liberals and feminists in this country began to argue that marriage that could not be ended by divorce was old-fashioned and tyrannical. The idea of marriage as a lifelong commitment began to come under fire on this side of the Atlantic.

CHANGING STATUS OF WIVES

In the early days of America, following English tradition, marriage signified the merger of husband and wife into one legal entity. The husband had the right of control and the duty of protecting the entity. The wife lacked a legal existence outside this unit.

Based on the theory of "unity of spouses," the husband had

the duty of support of the wife, and the responsibility for the debts she brought into the marriage. A husband and wife had no right to contract with each other; nor could the wife enter into a contract with a third party. She could not sue on her own behalf, or be sued without the joinder of her husband to the action.

The wife's legal existence, and often her entire identity, was merged into that of her husband. She was totally subordinate to his status as head of the household. Her status was almost one of servant; she was obliged to perform domestic duties appropriate to her station without compensation. When women began to question their legal status as wives, marriage would never be the same.

SEEDS OF CHANGE

As our country grew, the formation of families was facilitated by its limitless opportunities. Couples could marry young and form their own households. The "extended families" that were an economic necessity in the old country were no longer needed. Economic progress meant that romantic love, not practicality, would gradually become the basis for marriage "till death do us part."

The Industrial Revolution was also a major event that set in motion the changes that would affect the American family for years to come. Men were drawn away from their farms, with the result that families became less insular. World War II was responsible for another wave of change, as women entered the work force in droves, leaving behind their traditional roles as "just" homemakers. The new status of wives and mothers as wage earners led women to a reevaluation of their legal status in the matrimonial arena.

The effects of the Industrial Revolution and World War II, disparate events separated by several generations, were not immediately apparent. Although the divorce rate began to rise at the beginning of the century, it rose so gradually that no one really noticed. Following a brief increase after World War II, the divorce rate leveled off and Americans embraced the 1950s family-oriented ideal.

The baby boomers, heirs to many changes, began their lives in traditional nuclear families. The effects of progress, however, were about to catch up with the American family.

IN FULL BLOOM

Progress would bring:

- The Pill
- Urbanization
- Continued changes in the traditional roles of the sexes
- A rise in the percentage of the population pursuing a college education, leading to later marriages
- Studies that show marriage creates happier and healthier husbands than bachelorhood, but show that single women are happier and healthier than wives
- A decreasing birth rate
- The continued recognition of the legal rights of illegitimate children and the lessening of prejudice toward them
- An alarming divorce rate

THE DIVORCE REVOLUTION

Following the "free love" philosophy espoused in the 1960s, the old system of finding "fault" in the end of a marriage became passé. California, as is so often the case, broke new ground in 1970 with the concept of "no-fault" divorce.

Before this revolutionary idea, divorce was obtained only by proving adultery, cruelty, or abandonment. Unless there was mutual consent, proving one or the other of these charges was expensive and complicated.

Today, nearly all fifty states have some form of "no-fault" or "irreconcilable differences" divorce. Many marriages that might have survived the rigorous requirements of divorce in the past were no match for "divorce on demand."

THE TWO-PRONGED EFFECT

Today, our progressive society attaches little social stigma to divorce and it is easily obtained. The trend is toward shorter marriages, with a resulting younger age at divorce and subsequent remarriage. The combination of the divorce rate with the remarriage rate creates a two-pronged effect. First, divorce creates a large pool of unattached and available former spouses with a need and desire for remarriage who do not necessarily limit themselves to the unmarried. Second, spouses dissatisfied with a current marriage now have a greater assortment of potential spouses because the pool includes the never-married and the previously married. The "grass is greener" syndrome can lead to divorce in a cause-and-effect game of musical spouses.

DIVORCE TRENDS

Because of the decreasing birth rate and a trend toward smaller families, couples today spend fewer years concentrating on child rearing. An empty nest creates new and different strains on both partners, suddenly faced with fulfilling the other's needs and desires without the demands of a family. Add to these factors a longer life expectancy. When people live longer, there is a restructuring of families by divorce and remarriage that might once have occurred after one partner's death.

Biology may also be a big piece of the puzzle. Helen E. Fisher, an anthropologist at the American Museum of Natural History, looked at census data collected since 1947 from a variety of cultures. She found a pattern of three divorce peaks in societies throughout the world, though the cultures had few other similarities. The three peaks Dr. Fisher documented were among—

- Couples married four years
- Couples between ages twenty-five and twenty-nine
- Couples with no children or only one child

Because of the differences in the cultures, Fisher hypothesized that biology was the dominant factor in divorce, not influences and pressures from society. This study also documented that infatuation and its accompanying feelings of euphoria may be related to increased levels of brain stimulants. A tolerance to these stimulants builds up over several years and may be responsible for the four-year peak in divorce rates.

The modern tendency to divorce between the ages of twenty-five and twenty-nine may be linked to the instinct for survival of the species. The more freedom our earliest ancestors had during this peak reproductive period, the greater their ability to bear genetically varied offspring capable of surviving in greater numbers. Possibly, these survivors passed along their parents' restlessness in a long relationship, along with the continued optimism our species exhibits at the thought of the next romance.

Perhaps humans have simply never been mature enough for lifetime marriages. With our increasing life expectancy and our decreasing birth rate, couples find themselves going through stages that our ancestors may never have experienced.

REMARRIAGE

The previously married bride or groom has different needs than the young couple embarking on a first marriage. The responsibilities and obligations from prior marriages, particularly when children are involved, cannot be ignored.

Unfortunately, because of these concerns, there are more strains on a remarriage, particularly when children from prior marriages must be "reconstituted" into a family. Suddenly, there are two sets of fathers or mothers, four sets of grandparents, and assorted siblings and half-siblings.

Men and women who have children, whether they are the custodial parent or not, fight an uphill battle to define and fulfill their obligations regarding visitation, custody, support, and inheritance. These problems create stress for the old family, as well as the new.

Even without children, it is possible that obligations to former spouses will continue even after a marriage ends. Issues such as alimony, life and medical insurance, retirement benefits and pension rights, and shared investments in business or other property can interfere with the financial obligations of a new marriage. Balancing the demands of the new marriage with the leftover demands of the old requires special handling that the state's marriage contract may not provide.

SENIOR CITIZENS

The legal system, unfortunately, does not always make allowances for the needs of senior citizens who choose to marry. Childbearing and child-rearing questions are no longer an issue for these couples, but new issues replace these concerns.

Older couples must consider the potential loss of private pensions, alimony, social security benefits, and tax advantages because of a remarriage. Also important is the issue of inheritance of assets that may have taken a lifetime to accumulate (most likely with the help of a deceased spouse). The fact that older couples may want to limit their financial obligations to each other in the areas of support, medical costs, insurance, and pension benefits is of great concern.

SPOUSAL EQUIVALENTS

Marriage may be the only means of forming a legal and financial relationship under the law, but for many, legal marriage simply implies that they must suffer penalties to legalize their relationship.

As traditional marriage has proven less and less capable of living up to its potential in our society, alternatives such as unmarried cohabitation have arisen. The increase in couples who choose to cohabit can be traced to the fact that the marriage laws are not meeting the needs of these citizens in forming their personal relationships. Although there are a variety of reasons why couples choose to "just live together," financial disadvantages are a major factor.

The current laws in every state deny gay and lesbian couples the right of legal marriage. These couples have no choice but to remain outside the boundaries of conventional marriage, and have no means of legalizing their relationships.

SOCIETY'S NEW LEGAL ISSUES

The family offers the biological and social continuity that shapes, and is shaped by, our culture. The ever fluctuating needs of society reflect the changing demands of the many couples contemplating marriage today. While registering their china and silver patterns, today's couples cannot ignore the legal and financial demands of their new union.

The divorce laws and the laws relating to visitation, child support, and child custody continue to see major reforms throughout the country. No-fault divorce is available in nearly every state, but the freedom to obtain divorce more easily has not extended to new options being offered to those entering the marriage contract, although the ease of exiting from a legal marriage has contributed to remarriage and the widespread blended family. The one form of marriage in our country today struggles to meet the needs of those seeking to legalize their relationships.

THE LEGAL CHALLENGE OF CHANGE

American families today must also contend with unprecedented legal issues, including:

- The continued legalization of abortion
- Continuing research into new forms of contraception
- Artificial insemination
- Children's rights
- Surrogate motherhood
- In-vitro fertilization and embryo transplants
- Domestic violence

As our society faces these issues relating to marriage and family law, state involvement in the most personal of contracts is not only a reality but almost a necessity as we struggle for answers. The laws affecting our intimate relationships are not necessarily bad or intrusive in and of themselves. However, forming a marital relationship without considering all of the ramifications and without a working knowledge of the law can lead to situations in which the end result is both.

CAN THE LEGAL SYSTEM ADAPT?

Whether the legal system can address the issues facing couples in America today is unknown. The divorce laws have continued to evolve, so perhaps it is not unrealistic to expect that the marriage laws will as well.

Flexibility in our laws is clearly demanded to meet the needs of all members of our society. However, no matter what legislatures and courts decree, each couple who marries must take responsibility for their own relationship and its legal and financial ramifications. When issues are discussed, not ignored, and compromises are agreed to, marriages thrive. Beginning married life with this attitude is only practical. A premarital agreement may be the best wedding present yet. Taking an active role in structuring this new relationship is the best way for two to enjoy all of the benefits of becoming one.

APPENDIX A:
STATE LAWS

An overview of the law in each of the fifty states follows. Do not depend on the information in this appendix without consulting an attorney in your home state. Laws are subject to change and interpretation in each jurisdiction.

ALABAMA

Prohibited Marriages: Marriage is prohibited between individuals related either legitimately or illegitimately by blood or adoption; between a stepchild and stepparent, while the marriage creating the relationship exists; or between an aunt, nephew, or niece of the whole or half blood. Incest is a Class C felony.

Age of Consent: A person 18 years of age or older may consent to marry.

Consent Requirement: A person under 18 years of age who has not been previously married is required to have the written or oral consent of the parents or guardian.

License Requirement: A valid license issued by the judges of the several counties is required to solemnize the marriage. The license is valid for 30 days from the date of issuance.

Common-Law Marriages: Residents can enter into an informal marriage.

Annulment: A marriage may be annulled if it is incestuous or if one of the parties to the marriage is under the age of 14 years.

Theory of Marital Property: Separate.

Property Distribution upon Divorce: The court has the discretion to make allowance for a spouse (when there are insufficient funds for maintenance or if there has been misconduct) from the estate of the other spouse. This extends to the separate property acquired prior to marriage or by inheritance or gift if the separate property has been used regularly for the common benefit of the marriage. The court will make an equitable distribution of property based on (1) length of marriage; (2) source of property; (3) age, health, and station in life of parties; (4) contribution to the marriage; and (5) future prospects for acquisition of property and income. The court may consider the conduct of the parties as to the cause of divorce in determining a distribution.

Intestate Succession: WITH CHILDREN—(1) *Real.* If children are issue of spouse, spouse takes $50,000, plus ½ balance; children take residue. If children from a prior marriage, spouse takes ½; children take ½. (2) *Personal.* Same. NO CHILDREN—Spouse takes $100,000, plus ½ balance; parents take residue.

ALASKA

Prohibited Marriages: Marriage is prohibited if either party has a husband or a wife living, or if the parties are more closely related to each other than the fourth degree of consanguinity, whether of the whole blood or half blood, computed according to the rules of the civil law.

Age of Consent: A person 18 years of age or older may consent to marry.

Consent Requirement: A person 16 years of age will be issued a marriage license with parental consent. A superior judge may grant permission for a person under 14 years of age to marry with or without parental consent.

License Requirement: One of the parties to a prospective marriage must file with the licensing office an application for a license at least 3 days before the date of issuance. The license issued is valid for 3 months from the date of issuance.

Common-Law Marriages: Not recognized.

Annulment: Grounds for annulment include (1) failure to consummate marriage, (2) consent obtained by fraud or force, (3) party is of unsound mind, and (4) minors married without lawful consent. Children born of an annulled marriage are legitimate.

Theory of Marital Property: Separate.

Property Distribution Upon Divorce: Joint or separate property acquired during the marriage shall be divided in a "just" manner without regard to fault. The court may divide real or personal property acquired before the marriage when the balancing of the equities between the parties requires it.

Intestate Succession: WITH CHILDREN—(1) *Real.* If children are issue of spouse, spouse takes $50,000 plus ½ residue; children take residue. If children are from a prior marriage, spouse takes ½; children take ½. (2) *Personal.* Same. NO CHILDREN—Parents take residue. If no parents, brothers and sisters and their issue take residue.

ARIZONA

Prohibited Marriages: Marriages between parents and children, including grandparents and grandchildren of every degree; between brothers and sisters of the half or the whole blood; between uncles and nieces, and between aunts and nephews; and between first cousins are prohibited and void. However, cousins may marry if 65 years of age or older or if they can submit proof to judge that one cannot reproduce.

Age of Consent: A person 18 years of age or older may consent to marry.

Consent Requirement: Persons under 18 may not marry without the consent of a parent or guardian AND the approval of a superior court judge in the state.

License Requirement: In order to obtain a license to marry, the parties must file with the clerk of the superior court an oath declaring their names and ages, their places of residence, and their relationship.

Common-Law Marriages: Not recognized.

Annulment: A marriage may be annulled by a superior court judge on any ground constituting an impediment that renders the marriage void. The court, to the extent that it has jurisdiction to do so, shall establish the rights and obligations of the parties with respect to children in the same manner as in a divorce.

Theory of Marital Property: Community.

Property Distribution Upon Divorce: Community property is distributed equitably regardless of marital misconduct. Each spouse's sole and separate property is awarded to that spouse unless necessary to satisfy a judgment for child support or spousal maintenance. Property acquired outside the state is deemed community property if it would have been such if acquired within the state. The increase from separate property remains separate property.

Intestate Succession: WITH CHILDREN—(1) *Real.* Spouse takes everything, unless the deceased had children from another marriage. In that event, spouse takes all community and ½ separate, and children take residue. (2) *Personal.* Same.

ARKANSAS

Prohibited Marriages: Marriages between a parent and child, between grandparents and grandchildren, between brothers and sisters of the half blood as well as the whole blood, between uncles and nieces, between aunts and nephews, and between first cousins are incestuous and void.

Age of Consent: A person 18 years of age or older may consent to marry.

Consent Requirement: Parental consent or consent of guardian is required to marry if the male is age 17 and the female is age 16.

License Requirement: A notice of intention to wed, valid for 1 year after issuance and signed by both applicants, must be filed with the county clerk together with payment of the prescribed fee. In addition, a bond of $100 must be posted, which is returned once the marriage has taken place.

Common-Law Marriages: Not recognized.

Annulment: Grounds for annulment include (1) lack of physical capacity to consummate marriage, (2) consent obtained by fraud or force, (3) minor married without lawful consent, (4) and party lacked mental capacity to consent. Children born of an annulled marriage are legitimate.

Theory of Marital Property: Separate.

Property Distribution upon Divorce: All property acquired during the marriage is divided equally between the spouses unless the court determines an equal division is inequitable. The following factors will be considered: (1) the contribution of each spouse to the acquisition of the marital property, including the contribution of each spouse as homemaker; (2) length of the marriage; (3) age, health, and station in life of the parties; (4) the occupation of the parties; (5) the amount and sources of income of the parties; (6) vocational skills and employability of the parties; (7) estate, liabilities, and needs of each party and opportunity of each for further acquisition of capital assets and income; and (8) the federal income tax consequences of the court's division of the property. Fault may also be considered. The division may encompass nonmarital property under the factors set out previously. Property excluded from the definition of marital property includes any property excluded in a valid agreement of the parties or any property acquired prior to marriage, by gift or inheritance, a workers' compensation claim, or personal injury claim for any degree of permanent disability or future medical care during the marriage.

Intestate Succession: WITH CHILDREN—(1) *Real.* Spouse takes life estate in ⅓; children take remainder. (2) *Personal.* Spouse takes ⅓; children take residue. NO CHILDREN—Spouse takes all unless married less than three years. In that event, spouse takes ½ and parents take ½. If parents are deceased, brothers and sisters and their issue take ½.

CALIFORNIA

Prohibited Marriages: Marriages between parents and children, ancestors and descendants of every degree, between brothers and sisters of the whole or half blood, between uncles and nieces, and between aunts and nephews are incestuous and void. Bigamous and polygamous marriages are also void.

Age of Consent: A person 18 years of age or older may consent to marry.

Consent Requirement: A person under 18 years of age may marry with the written consent of the parent(s) or guardian, an order of the superior court granting permission, and proof that the parties have participated in premarital counseling, if the court deems such counseling necessary.

License Requirement: A license issued by the county clerk is required. An unmarried man and an unmarried woman, not minors, who have been cohabiting as husband and wife may, without obtaining a license, be married by any person authorized to solemnize a marriage. An authorization for the performance of such a marriage may be issued by the county clerk, the clerk of the court, or a judge in private chambers upon the personal appearance of the parties to be married and payment of the required fees. Said authorization is valid for 90 days from the date of issuance and can only be used in the county in which it was issued.

Common-Law Marriages: Not recognized.

Annulment: Grounds for annulment include (1) bigamy, (2) lack of physical capacity to consummate marriage, (3) consent obtained by fraud, (4) party is of unsound mind, (5) and minor married without lawful consent.

Theory of Marital Property: Community.

Property Distribution upon Divorce: Unless the parties agree otherwise, community property and quasi-community property (property acquired elsewhere that would have been community if acquired in California) are divided equally between the parties. Court may make an offsetting award if a party has deliberately misappropriated property. Spouse shall be reimbursed for separate property contributions to the community, unless this right is waived in writing. Community debt in excess of assets may be awarded unequally based on ability to pay. Community contributions to the education or training of a party that substantially increase or enhance that party's earning capacity are reimbursable to the community.

Intestate Succession: Effective July of 1991, the community property of the deceased spouse would go in equal shares to the nearest generation of issue living. The issue of any deceased member of that generation would inherit that share in equal shares.

COLORADO

Prohibited Marriages: Marriages that are prohibited are bigamous marriage; marriages between ancestors and descendants or between brothers and sisters, whether the relationship is by the half or the whole blood or by adoption; marriages between uncles and nieces and nieces or aunts and nephews, whether by half or whole blood, *except* if permitted by established customs or aboriginal cultures.

Age of Consent: A person 18 years of age or older may consent to marry.

Consent Requirement: A person over the age of 16 but under 18 years of age may enter into marriage with the consent of both parents or the guardian. If the parents are not living together, the parent who has legal custody or with whom the child is living or the juvenile court may consent. If the child is under 16 years of age, the consent of both parents, or the guardian, is required. If the parents are living apart, the parent who has legal custody or with whom the child is living *and* the consent of the juvenile court are necessary.

License Requirement: When a marriage application has been completed and signed by both parties and at least one of the parties appears before the county clerk and pays a license fee, the license clerk shall issue a license to marry and a marriage certificate. Before a license is issued, each applicant shall file a certificate from a licensed physician. The license issued shall not be valid for more than 30 days.

Common-Law Marriages: Residents can enter into informal marriages.

Annulment: Grounds for annulment include (1) bigamy, (2) fraud, (3) lack of physical capacity to consummate marriage, (4) consent obtained by fraud or duress, (5) minor married without lawful consent, (6) party lacked mental capacity to consent (including temporary incapacity resulting from drug or alcohol use), (7) one or both entered into marriage as a jest or dare, and (8) incest. Children born of an annulled marriage are legitimate.

Theory of Marital Property: Separate.

Property Distribution upon Divorce: Courts will distribute marital property equitably, without regard to marital misconduct. Property owned before marriage, and gifted and inherited property, are excluded, except as to increased value. Marital property is defined as all property acquired by either spouse after the marriage, regardless of whether title is held individually or in some form of co-ownership. Factors to be considered in an equitable division are (1) contribution of each spouse to the acquisition of the marital property, including the contribution of a spouse as homemaker; (2) value of the property set apart to each spouse; (3) economic circumstances of each spouse at the time of the effective division of property, including the desirability of awarding the family home or right to live therein to the spouse with custody of the children; (4) any increases or decreases in the value of the separate property of the spouse during marriage; and (5) the depletion of the separate property for marital purposes.

Intestate Succession: WITH CHILDREN—(1) *Real.* If children are issue of spouse, spouse takes $25,000 plus ½ balance; children take residue. If children from a prior marriage, spouse takes ½ and children take ½. (2) *Personal.* Same. NO CHILDREN—Spouse takes all.

CONNECTICUT

Prohibited Marriages: Marriage between a man and his mother, grandmother, daughter, granddaughter, sister, aunt, niece, stepmother, or stepdaughter and between a woman and her father, grandfather, son, grandson, brother, uncle, nephew, stepfather, or stepson are incestuous and prohibited. Any child born by a void or voidable marriage is legitimate.

Age of Consent: A person 18 years of age or older may consent to marry.

Consent Requirement: Persons under 18 years of age may marry with parental consent or consent of the judge of probate; persons under 16 years of age may marry only with the consent of the judge of probate.

License Requirement: A marriage license issued by the registrar for the town in which the marriage is to be celebrated is required. The license will not be issued unless a premarital certificate signed by a licensed physician has been filed with the registrar. There is a 4-day waiting period governing the issuance of marriage licenses. The license is valid for 65 days.

Common-Law Marriages: Not recognized.

Annulment: If a marriage is prohibited or voidable, it will be annulled either under the laws of Connecticut or under the laws of the state in which the marriage was performed.

Theory of Marital Property: Separate.

Property Distribution upon Divorce: The court may assign to either spouse all or any part of the estate of the other. Fault is one of the factors considered in the division of property. Other factors considered are the following: (1) length of the marriage; (2) causes for the divorce; (3) age, health, station, and occupation; (4) amounts and sources of income; (5) vocational skills; (6) employability; (7) estate; (8) liabilities and needs of parties; and (9) opportunity for each for future acquisition of assets and income. The court will also consider the contribution of each of the parties in the acquisition and appreciation of the estates.

Intestate Succession: WITH CHILDREN—(1) *Real.* Spouse takes $50,000 plus ½ of residue; children take residue, unless there are surviving children of a previous marriage. Then, spouse takes ½; children take ½. (2) *Personal.* Same. NO CHILDREN—Spouse takes $5,000 plus ¾ of residue; parents take other ¼.

DELAWARE

Prohibited Marriages: Marriage between a person and his or her ancestor, descendant, brother, sister, uncle, aunt, niece, nephew, or first cousin are incestuous and prohibited. Also prohibited are marriage to a person who is of unsound mind, marriage to a patient in a mental hospital unless the patient files a certificate signed by the superintendent of the mental hospital that such a person is fit to marry, marriage to one suffering a venereal disease unknown to the other party, marriage to a habitual drunkard or confirmed drug addict, marriage to a divorced person unless a certified copy of the divorce decree is inspected by the clerk of the court, marriage to a person on probation or on parole unless such person files with the clerk of the court a written consent to the proposed marriage signed by the probation officer or parole officer, and marriage between paupers. Children of void or voidable marriages are legitimate.

Age of Consent: A male 18 years of age or older, and a female 16 years or older, may enter into a valid marriage.

Consent Requirement: Females under 18 years of age may not marry without parental or guardian consent. However, any person under the legal age may marry if he or she acknowledges under oath that he or she is the parent or prospective parent of a child.

License Requirement: Persons wishing to marry must obtain a license valid for 30 days from the date of issuance. If one or both of the parents are residents of the state, they must obtain the license at least 24 hours before the ceremony. If neither party resides in the state, they must obtain the license at least 96 hours before the ceremony.

Common-Law Marriages: Not recognized.

Annulment: Grounds for annulment include (1) lack of physical capacity to consummate marriage; (2) consent obtained by fraud, duress, or force; (3) minor married without lawful consent; (4) party lacked mental capacity to consent (including temporary incapacity resulting from drug or alcohol use); and (5) one or both entered into marriage as a jest or dare.

Theory of Marital Property: Separate.

Property Distribution upon Divorce: Marital property is divided equitably between the parties without regard to marital misconduct. In making such a division the court considers the following factors: (1) length of the marriage; (2) any prior marriage of the party; (3) age, health, and station in life of the parties; (4) whether the property award is in lieu of or in addition to alimony; (5) the opportunities of each for further acquisition of assets or income; (6) the contribution of each spouse to the acquisition of the marital property, including the contribution of each spouse as homemaker; (7) the value of the property set apart to each party; (8) the economic circumstances of each spouse at the time the division of property is to become effective; (9) whether the property was acquired by gift, devise, or descent; (10) debts of the parties; and (11) tax consequences of the court's division of the property. Property may be excluded by valid agreement of the parties.

Intestate Succession: WITH CHILDREN—(1) *Real.* Spouse takes life estate; children take remainder. (2) *Personal.* If children are issue of spouse, spouse takes $50,000 plus ½ balance; children take residue. If children from a prior marriage, spouse takes ½; children take ½. NO CHILDREN—Spouse has life estate in real property and $50,000 plus ½ of personal property; parents take residue.

DISTRICT OF COLUMBIA

Prohibited Marriages: Marriages between a person and a grandparent, grandparent's spouse, spouse's grandparent, aunt, uncle, parent or stepparent, spouse's parent, child, child's spouse, sibling, sibling's child, sibling's child's spouse, or spouse's child's child are prohibited and null and void. Bigamous marriages are likewise prohibited.

Age of Consent: A person 16 years of age or older may consent to marry.

Consent Requirement: Persons who are under 18 years of age and who have not been previously married may not marry without the consent of a parent or guardian.

License Requirement: In order to obtain a license to marry, the parties must state under oath on a printed application their names, the names of their parents or guardians if the parties are underage, whether they were previously married, and whether and in what degree they are related. After the application has been submitted, there is a 3-day waiting period before the license may be issued. No application for a marriage license will be received without a physician's statement that the applicant has submitted to a laboratory blood test within the previous 30 days and does not have infectious syphilis. A judge of the superior court may waive certain license provisions for reasons of public policy or physical condition of either of the applicants.

Common-Law Marriages: Residents can enter into an informal marriage.

Annulment: Grounds for annulment include (1) bigamy, (2) lack of physical capacity to consummate marriage, (3) consent obtained by fraud or force, (4) party is of unsound mind, and (5) minor married without lawful consent.

Theory of Marital Property: Separate.

Property Distribution upon Divorce: Courts must divide marital property in a manner that is equitable, just, and reasonable. Property acquired prior to marriage or by gift or inheritance (and its increase in value) are exempt from distribution. In the absence of a valid marital agreement, the court will distribute property regardless of the title, after considering such factors as (1) duration of marriage and any prior marriages; (2) age, health, and occupation; (3) amounts and sources of income; (4) vocational skills, employability, assets, debts, needs of parties, and provisions for custody of minor children; (4) opportunity of each for future acquisition of assets and income; and (5) contribution to the value of the assets and contribution of homemaker to the family unit.

Intestate Succession: WITH CHILDREN—(1) *Real.* Spouse takes ⅓; children take residue. (2) *Personal.* Spouse takes ⅓; children take residue. NO CHILDREN—Spouse takes ½; parents take ½. If parents are deceased, brothers and sisters or their issue take ½.

FLORIDA

Prohibited Marriages: Bigamous and incestuous marriages are prohibited. An incestuous marriage is a marriage between two persons related by lineal consanguinity or a marriage between a person and his sister, aunt, or niece; or her brother, uncle, or nephew. Persons entering into either a bigamous or an incestuous marriage are guilty of a felony in the third degree.

Age of Consent: A person 18 years of age or older may consent to marry.

Consent Requirement: Persons under age 18 but at least 16 years of age can marry with the consent of their parents or guardian, but no such consent is required when both parents are deceased or when the minor has been previously married or when the minors are the parents of a child or are expecting a child.

License Requirement: Before a license to marry is granted, the parties must file with the county clerk an affidavit stating their true and correct ages and a health certificate from a licensed physician. The license is valid for 30 days from the date of issuance.

Common-Law Marriages: Not recognized.

Annulment: There is no relevant statutory provision.

Theory of Marital Property: Separate.

Property Distribution upon Divorce: The courts will grant an equitable distribution of marital assets, regardless of the title. Equitable distribution does not require an equal division, but the goal is equity and justice between the parties, based on (1) the contribution of each spouse to the acquisition of the marital property, including the contribution of each spouse as homemaker; (2) duration of the marriage; (3) economic circumstances; (4) contribution to the acquisition, enhancement, and improvement of the assets; and (5) liabilities of the parties.

Intestate Succession: WITH CHILDREN—(1) *Real.* If children are issue of spouse, spouse takes $20,000 plus ½ balance; children take residue. If children from prior marriage, spouse takes ½ and children take ½. (2) *Personal.* Same. NO CHILDREN—Spouse takes all.

GEORGIA

Prohibited Marriages: Bigamous marriages are prohibited. Marriages between father and daughter or stepdaughter; mother and son or stepson; brother and sister of the whole or half blood; grandparent and grandchild; aunt and nephew; or uncle and niece are prohibited.

Age of Consent: A person over 16 years of age may marry without parental consent. If there is proof of pregnancy or both applicants are the parents of a living child born out of wedlock, they may marry regardless of age.

Consent Requirement: Parental consent is required if either party is under 16 years of age. Parental consent means the consent of both parents if they are living together, the consent of the parent with legal custody if the parents are divorced or separated, the consent of either parent if they are living together but one is unavailable because he or she is ill or because physical presence is impossible, or the consent of the legal guardian.

License Requirement: A license, issued by the judge of the probate court or by the judge's clerk, is required. An application for a license to be filed in the office of the judge of the probate court is required. Each person who applies for a license is required to present a physician's certificate.

Common-Law Marriages: Residents may enter into an informal marriage.

Annulment: Any marriage void by law may be annulled. The code provides that any child born before the marriage is annulled shall be legitimate, while at the same time prohibiting annulments in instances where children are born or are to be born. In cases of minors or mental incompetents, a guardian may file for annulment on their behalf. The Georgia Supreme Court has denied annulments in instances where children are involved; parties to such marriage must file for divorce. In addition, where grounds for annulment and divorce overlap, the court may only permit a divorce as a remedy.

Theory of Marital Property: Separate.

Property Distribution upon Divorce: Georgia does not have a specific statute governing the division of property upon divorce, but a court may effectuate an equitable distribution of property through the state's alimony statute. Fault may be considered.

Intestate Succession: WITH CHILDREN—(1) *Real*. Wife takes equal share with children but no less than ⅕; husband takes equal share. (2) *Personal*. Same. NO CHILDREN—Spouse takes all.

HAWAII

Prohibited Marriages: Marriages between ancestors and descendants of any degree whatsoever, brother and sister of the half or whole blood, uncle and niece, or aunt and nephew, whether the relationship is legitimate or illegitimate are incestuous and void. Children born of void marriages are legitimate.

Age of Consent: A person 18 years of age or older may consent to marry.

Consent Requirement: A person under the age of 18 may marry with parental or guardian consent. If under age 16, approval of the family court of the circuit within which the minor resides is required.

License Requirement: A person wishing to marry must apply personally for a marriage license, which is valid for 30 days from the date of issuance. The female applicant for a marriage license must show proof of immunization against rubella.

Common-Law Marriages: Not recognized.

Annulment: Grounds for annulment include (1) bigamy, (2) minor married without lawful consent, (3) party lacked mental capacity to consent, (4) incest, and (5) one party suffers from a loathsome disease unknown to the other.

Theory of Marital Property: Separate.

Property Distribution upon Divorce: The court will distribute the property of the parties, whether community, joint, or separate, in a just manner, taking into account the respective merits of the parties, the relative abilities of the parties, the condition in which each party will be left by the divorce, the burdens imposed upon either party for the benefit of the children of the parties, and all other circumstances of the case.

Intestate Succession: WITH CHILDREN—Spouse has dower or curtesy rights in ⅓ of the property; children take residue. NO

CHILDREN—Spouse takes ½; parents take ½. If parents are deceased, brothers and sisters and their issue take ½.

IDAHO

Prohibited Marriages: Marriages between parents and children, between ancestors and descendants of every degree, between brothers and sisters of the half as well as the whole blood, and between uncles and nieces or aunts and nephews are incestuous and void from the beginning whether the relationship is legitimate or illegitimate. Marriages between first cousins are prohibited. Children of void or prohibited marriages are legitimate unless the wife was pregnant with the child of a man other than the husband.

Age of Consent: An unmarried person over 18 years of age, not otherwise disqualified, may consent to marry.

Consent Requirement: A person under 18 years of age and over 16 years of age may marry with written parental consent. Anyone under 16 years of age may marry with written parental consent and upon order of the court.

License Requirement: A marriage license to be issued by the county recorder is required. The requirement of a medical certificate to receive a marriage license has been repealed.

Common-Law Marriages: Residents can enter into an informal marriage.

Annulment: Grounds for annulment include (1) bigamy, (2) lack of physical capacity to consummate marriage, (3) consent obtained by fraud or force, (4) party is of unsound mind, and (5) minor married without lawful consent.

Theory of Marital Property: Community.

Property Distribution upon Divorce: Unless there are compelling reasons, the court shall divide the community property substantially equally. The court will consider but will not be limited by the following factors: (1) length of the marriage; (2) any antenuptial agreement of the parties; (3) age, health, occupation, source of income, vocational skills, and employability of the parties, and liability of each spouse; (4) the needs of each spouse; (5) whether the apportionment is in lieu of or in addition to maintenance; (6) present and potential earning capability of each party; and (7) retirement benefits, including but not limited to social security, civil service, military, and railroad retirement benefits.

Intestate Succession: WITH CHILDREN—(1) *Real.* Community property all to spouse. Spouse takes $50,000 plus ½ balance; children take residue. If there are surviving children from a prior marriage, spouse takes ½; children take ½. (2) *Personal.* Same. NO CHILDREN—Parents take ½ separate property.

ILLINOIS

Prohibited Marriages: Bigamous marriages are prohibited. Marriages between an ancestor and a descendant, a brother and a sister (whether by the half or whole blood or by adoption), an uncle and a niece, an aunt and a nephew (whether by the half or whole blood), or first cousins, except for marriages between first cousins 50 years of age or older, are incestuous and void. Children born of void or prohibited marriages are legitimate.

Age of Consent: A person 18 years of age or older may consent to marry.

Consent Requirement: A person 16 years of age or older may marry with parental or guardian consent or judicial approval.

License Requirement: Persons intending to marry must obtain a license from the county clerk. The license is issued upon furnishing satisfactory proof that the parties are of age and that the marriage is not prohibited.

Common-Law Marriages: Not recognized.

Annulment: Grounds for declaring a marriage invalid include (1) bigamy; (2) lack of physical capacity to consummate marriage; (3) consent obtained by fraud, duress, or force; (4) party lacked mental capacity because of infirmity or influence of drugs or alcohol; (5) minor married without lawful consent; and (7) incest.

Theory of Marital Property: Separate.

Property Distribution upon Divorce: Nonmarital property includes any property classified as such in a valid agreement, property acquired by gift, or inheritance or any increase thereof. Marital property is subject to equitable distribution without regard to fault. The following factors are considered: (1) the contribution of each spouse to the acquisition of the marital property, including the contribution of each spouse as homemaker; (2) the value of property set apart for each spouse; (3) the duration of the marriage; (4) the economic circumstances of each spouse at the time the division of property is to become effective; (5) obligations arising from a prior marriage; (6) any antenuptial agreement; (7) age, health, occupation, and station in life of the parties; (8) custodial provisions for the children; (9) whether the property award is in lieu of or in addition to alimony; (10) opportunity of each for further acquisition of capital assets and income; and (11) tax consequences of the court's division of the property.

Intestate Succession: WITH CHILDREN—(1) *Real.* Spouse takes ⅓; children take ⅔. (2) *Personal.* Same. NO CHILDREN—Spouse takes all.

INDIANA

Prohibited Marriages: Bigamous marriages, marriages where one is of unsound mind, and marriages entered into by evading the laws of the state are void. Marriages between first cousins 65 years of age or older, entered into after September 1, 1977, are valid; otherwise, marriages between individuals more closely related than second cousins are prohibited. No legal proceedings are required to declare the nullity of a marriage prohibited by law. Children of void marriages entered into in good faith are legitimate.

Age of Consent: A person 18 years of age or older may consent to marry.

Consent Requirement: Individuals who are at least 17 years of age may marry with the written consent of a parent or guardian, signed and verified in the presence of the clerk of the circuit court. Individuals under age 18 may also petition the judge of the circuit or superior court of their county of residence to authorize the clerk of the court to issue a marriage license. Individuals under age 17 may also marry if the following circumstances are met: the female is at least 15 years of age and either pregnant or a mother, the male is the putative father of the child, both the male and the female have the written consent of their parents or guardians, and a judge of the circuit, superior, or county court of the residence of one of the parties authorizes the clerk of the circuit court to issue a marriage license.

License Requirement: Persons intending to marry must obtain a license from the clerk of the circuit court of the county in which either or both of the parties reside. If the parties are nonresidents of the state, they must obtain the license from the clerk of the circuit court in which the marriage ceremony is to be performed. There is a 3-day waiting period for the issuance of the license, which is valid for 60 days from the date of issuance. Individuals may petition the circuit or superior court to issue the marriage license when they apply for it. A premarital examination is required before the license is issued. A marriage license may not be issued if either party is of unsound mind, is under the influence of alcohol or narcotics, or has a transmissible disease.

Common-Law Marriages: Not recognized.

Annulment: A marriage is voidable if a party lacked mental capacity to consent or if consent was obtained by fraud.

Theory of Marital Property: Separate.

Property Distribution upon Divorce: The court may effect a just and reasonable distribution of property, whether jointly or separately owned or acquired before or after the marriage. The following factors are also considered: (1) the contribution to the acquisition of the marital property, including the contribution of each spouse as homemaker; (2) extent to which the property was acquired by each spouse prior to the marriage or through inheritance or gift; (3) the economic circumstances of each spouse at the time the division of property is to become effective; (4) the conduct of the parties during the marriage as it relates to the disposition of their property; (5) the earnings or earning ability of the parties; and (6) the tax consequences of the division.

Intestate Succession: WITH CHILDREN—(1) *Real.* Spouse takes ½ with one child, ⅓ with two or more; children take residue. (2) *Personal.* Same. NO CHILDREN—Spouse takes ¾; parents take ¼.

IOWA

Prohibited Marriages: Marriages between a man and his aunt, daughter, sister, grandchildren, or nieces are prohibited. Marriages between a woman and her uncle, son, brother, grandchildren, or nephews are prohibited. Children born of void marriages are legitimate.

Age of Consent: A person 18 years of age or older may consent to marry.

Consent Requirement: A minor 16 or 17 years of age may marry with parental or guardian consent and the approval of the district judge.

License Requirement: Persons wishing to marry must first obtain a license from the clerk of the district court. The license is issued 3 days from the date of application. The clerk of the district court is authorized to issue a marriage license to the parties to a proposed marriage under extraordinary circumstances.

Common-Law Marriages: Residents can enter into an informal marriage.

Annulment: Grounds for annulment include (1) marriages prohibited by law, (2) lack of physical capacity to consummate marriage, and (3) mental illness.

Theory of Marital Property: Separate.

Property Distribution upon Divorce: Property is subject to equitable distribution unless inherited or gifted. The court may consider (1) length of the marriage; (2) property brought to the marriage by each party; (3) contribution of each party to the marriage, giving value to contributions of homemaking and child care; (4) age and physical and emotional health of the parties; (5) contribution by one party to the education, training, or increased earning power of the other; (6) the earning capacity of each party; (7) desirability of awarding family home to party having custody of children; (8) amount and duration of support payments and whether division is in lieu of these payments; (9) other economic circumstances, such as pension benefits and future interests; (10) tax consequences of division; (11) any written agreement between the parties; (12) other factors relevant in an individual case, including the best interest of the children.

Intestate Succession: WITH CHILDREN—*Real and Personal.* Spouse takes all, unless children from a prior marriage; then spouse takes ½ real property, all personal property in the possession of the deceased as head of household, ½ other personal property, but no less than $50,000. NO CHILDREN—Spouse takes all.

KANSAS

Prohibited Marriages: All marriages between parents and children, including grandparents and grandchildren of any degree, between brothers and sisters of the half as well as the whole blood; and between uncles and nieces, aunts and nephews, and first cousins are incestuous and void. Children born of void marriages are legitimate.

Age of Consent: A person 18 years of age or older may consent to marry.

Consent Requirement: Persons under age 18 may marry with parental or guardian consent and approval of the district judge.

License Requirement: Persons wishing to marry must first obtain a marriage license from either a clerk or a judge of the district court. The license is issued 3 days from the date of application, and expires in six months.

Common-Law Marriages: Residents can enter into an informal marriage.

Annulment: Grounds for annulment include (1) a void or voidable marriage, including inducement by mistake of fact.

Theory of Marital Property: Separate.

Property Distribution upon Divorce: Property subject to equitable distribution includes property owned by either spouse before marriage, acquired by either spouse in the spouse's own right after marriage, or acquired by the spouses' joint efforts. In making the division, the court may consider (1) age of the parties; (2) duration of the marriage; (3) property owned by the parties; (4) present and future earning capacities; (5) time, source, and manner of acquisition of property; (6) family ties and obligations; (7) allowance of maintenance or lack thereof; (8) dissipation of assets; and (9) other factors necessary.

Intestate Succession: WITH CHILDREN—(1) *Real.* Spouse takes ½; children take ½. (2) *Personal.* Same. NO CHILDREN—Spouse takes all.

KENTUCKY

Prohibited Marriages: Marriages may not be contracted between persons who are closer in relationship than second cousins, whether by the whole or half blood. Polygamous marriages, bigamous marriages, marriages not solemnized by an authorized person or society, and marriages to persons adjudged mentally disabled by a court of competent jurisdiction are prohibited. However, except for polygamous marriages, a marriage valid in the state where contracted is valid in Kentucky. Children born of void marriages are legitimate.

Age of Consent: A person 18 years of age or older may consent to marry.

Consent Requirement: A person under 18 years of age may marry only with the consent of a parent, guardian, or other person legally responsible for him or her.

License Requirement: A license issued by the county clerk is required. There is no statutory requirement for a premarital examination. However, every physician examining an applicant for a marriage license may obtain specimens of their blood to be tested for the nonexistence of sickle-cell trait or any other genetically transmitted disease. When both parties are carriers of a trait or disease, genetic counseling may be provided. No marriage that has been solemnized is invalid for want of a marriage license if it is consummated with the belief of either or both parties that they have been lawfully married. A marriage license is valid for 30 days from the date of issuance.

Common-Law Marriages: Not recognized.

Annulment: Grounds for annulment include (1) bigamy; (2) underage; (3) party lacked mental capacity to consent, including temporary incapacity resulting from drug or alcohol use; and (5) marriage not authorized in the presence of a person authorized to conduct marriages.

Theory of Marital Property: Separate.

Property Distribution upon Divorce: The court shall divide marital property without regard to marital misconduct and in just proportions. Factors considered are (1) homemaker's contribution, (2) value of properties set apart, (3) duration of marriage, and (4) economic circumstances of each spouse. Excluded from marital property are property acquired by gift, bequest, devise, or descent; property acquired in exchange for property acquired before marriage or by gift, and the like; property acquired after legal separation; an increase in value of property acquired before the marriage that was not a result of joint efforts; and property excluded by valid agreement.

Intestate Succession: WITH CHILDREN—(1) *Real.* Spouse takes dower or curtesy rights; children take residue. (2) *Personal.* Spouse takes $7,500; children take remainder. NO CHILDREN—Spouse takes dower or curtesy plus $7,500 of personal property; parents take residue of personal property. If parents deceased, brothers and sisters or their issue take residue and residue of personal property.

LOUISIANA

Prohibited Marriages: Bigamous marriages and marriages between parent and child, brother and sister, aunt and nephew, niece and uncle, and first cousins are prohibited, either by consanguinity or adoption. Children born of void marriages are legitimate.

Age of Consent: A person 21 years of age or older may consent to marry.

Consent Requirement: A minor over age 18 but under age 21 must obtain the consent of one or both parents or, if they are both dead, of his or her tutor and the oath of two persons 21 years of age or older that the applicants are the ages they represent themselves to be. Judges with jurisdiction over the juvenile court may grant permission for underage applicants to marry.

License Requirement: Licenses are issued by the Board of Health and by judges of the city courts in the parish of Orleans and by clerks of the courts in all other parishes. Where the clerk is a party to the marriage, the license is issued by the district judge. Before issuance of such license, both parties to the marriage must file with the license-issuing authority certified copies of their birth certificates and medical certificates, dated within 10 days of the license application, certifying that they do not have a venereal disease. There is a 12-hour waiting period before the marriage can be performed. However, the court may waive this waiting period for meritorious reasons.

Common-Law Marriages: Not recognized.

Annulment: Grounds for annulment include (1) bigamy; (2) consent obtained by fraud, duress, or force; and (3) incest.

Theory of Marital Property: Community.

Property Distribution upon Divorce: Community property is divided equally. Assets and liabilities will be divided so that each receives property of an equal net value.

Intestate Succession: WITH CHILDREN—(1) *Real.* Spouse has life estate; children take remainder. (2) *Personal.* Same. NO CHILDREN —Spouse takes ½; parents take ½.

MAINE

Prohibited Marriages: Marriages between parents and children, sisters and brothers, grandparents and grandchildren, aunts and nephews, and nieces and uncles are prohibited. With genetic counseling, first cousins may marry. Persons who are mentally ill or mentally retarded to the extent that they lack the mental capacity to make decisions about their property or person may not marry. Polygamous marriages are void. Children born of marriages that have been annulled because of consanguinity or affinity of the parties are illegitimate. However, children born of marriages annulled because of nonage or mental illness are legitimate.

Age of Consent: A person 18 years of age or older may consent to marry.

Consent Requirement: A child under 18 years of age must have the written consent of his or her parents, guardian, or, in their absence, the judge of probate of the county in which the child resides. In the case of a child under 16 years of age, the written consent of his or her parents, guardian, or court-appointed guardian and of the judge of probate is required.

License Requirement: A valid license will be issued by the clerk of the town in which each party resides, or of an adjoining town if there is no clerk in their place of residence, three days after filing notice. In the case of out-of-state residents, the clerk in the town in which they intend to marry shall issue the license. A marriage license is void if not used within 90 days from the date intentions to marry are filed.

Common-Law Marriages: Not recognized.

Annulment: Grounds for annulment include (1) bigamy, (2) unsound mind, and (3) incest. A marriage may be annulled when there is doubt about its validity upon the filing of complaint as if for divorce.

Theory of Marital Property: Separate.

Property Distribution upon Divorce: Excluded from marital property are inherited or gifted property, and the increase in value of property acquired before marriage. The court considers the following factors: (1) the contribution of each spouse to the acquisition of the marital property, including the contribution of each spouse as homemaker; (2) the value of property set aside to each party; and (3) the economic circumstances of each spouse at the time the division of property is to become effective.

Intestate Succession: WITH CHILDREN—(1) *Real.* Spouse takes first $50,000 plus ½; children take remainder unless children from prior marriage. Then, spouse takes ½; children take ½. (2) *Personal.* Same. NO CHILDREN—Spouse takes $50,000 plus ½ remaining real property and ½ personal property; parents take residue.

MARYLAND

Prohibited Marriages: Marriage between a person and his or her parent, grandparent, child, sister, brother, aunt, uncle, niece, nephew, grandchild, son-in-law, daughter-in-law, stepchild, stepparent, stepgrandparent, grandchild's spouse, spouse's grandchild, mother-in-law, father-in-law, or grandparent-in-law are prohibited.

Bigamous marriages are also prohibited. Children born of void or prohibited marriages are legitimate.

Age of Consent: A person 18 years of age or older may consent to marry.

Consent Requirement: Persons under age 16 must have the consent of a parent or guardian and either party must provide the clerk with certified proof from a licensed physician that the woman to be married is pregnant or has given birth to a child. Persons 16 or 17 years old must have either the consent of a parent or guardian, who must swear that the individual is at least 16 years old, or a medical certificate from a licensed physician stating that the woman to be married is pregnant or has given birth to a child.

License Requirement: A license issued by the county clerk is required in order to marry.

Common-Law Marriages: Not recognized.

Annulment: Grounds for annulment include (1) bigamy and (2) incurable mental illness.

Theory of Marital Property: Separate.

Property Distribution upon Divorce: The court may not transfer the ownership of property from one spouse to another but may grant a monetary award as an adjustment of the equities and rights of the parties. Marital property is all property except that acquired prior to marriage, by inheritance or gift from a third party, or property excluded by valid agreement. The court will consider (1) the contribution of each spouse to the well-being of the family; (2) the value of all property interest of each party; (3) the economic circumstances of each party; (4) circumstances that contributed to estrangement; (5) duration of marriage; (6) age of each party; (7) physical and mental condition of each party; (8) how and when marital property was acquired, including effort expended by each party; (9) any award of alimony; and (10) any other factor appropriate in arriving at a fair and equitable monetary award.

Intestate Succession: WITH CHILDREN—(1) *Real.* Spouse takes ½; minor children take ½. When children are grown, spouse takes $15,000 plus ½; children take residue. (2) *Personal.* Same. NO CHILDREN—Spouse takes $15,000 plus ½; parents take residue.

MASSACHUSETTS

Prohibited Marriages: No person may marry his or her parent, grandparent, child, grandchild, sibling, stepparent, grandparent's spouse, grandchild's spouse, spouse's parent, spouse's grandparent, spouse's child, spouse's grandchild, or parent's sibling. A marriage contracted where either party has a living spouse is void. A marriage contracted in good faith, where the original spouse is wrongfully presumed dead or divorced, is valid, provided a legal divorce is then secured from the original spouse. A marriage solemnized in Massachusetts but prohibited by reason of either incest or bigamy is void without a judgment of divorce or other legal process. Children born of incestuous marriages are illegitimate. However, children born of marriages declared void by reason of the nonage, insanity, or idiocy of either party are legitimate. Children born of bigamous marriages contracted in good faith are legitimate.

Age of Consent: Persons 18 years of age or older may give consent to marry.

Consent Requirement: A minor may marry with the consent of both parents or the surviving parent, or if only one parent resides in the commonwealth, that parent. Notice of the proceeding will be sent to the parent residing outside of the commonwealth.

License Requirement: Persons wishing to marry must obtain a certificate permitting the marriage from the clerk or registrar of any city or town in the commonwealth. The certificate is issued between 3 and 60 days after filing a notice of intention to marry. The certificate will be issued only when each party has provided a medical certificate from a doctor who has conducted a test for syphilis not more than 30 days before the filing of the notice of intention to marry or not more than 60 days before the issuance of the certificate. A medical certificate certifying that the female has been protected against rubella or is informed about the dangers of not being protected is also required. (This provision does not apply where the female cannot conceive.) The medical certificates can be waived where the death of either party is imminent, where the female is in the advanced stage of pregnancy, or where a waiver has been requested by a member of the clergy or a physician.

Common-Law Marriages: Not recognized.

Annulment: Where the validity of a marriage is doubted, either party may institute an action for annulling or affirming the marriage. The action is instituted in the same manner as divorce, and all provisions relevant to divorce apply.

Theory of Marital Property: Separate.

Property Distribution upon Divorce: The court may assign all or part of the estate of either spouse to the other. The court may consider (1) duration of marriage; (2) age, health, and station of each party; (3) amount and source of income; (4) vocational skills; (5) employability; (6) the value of all property interest of each party; (7) liabilities and needs of each party; (8) circumstances that contributed to estrangement; (9) opportunities for future acquisition or assets and income, and any other factor appropriate in arriving at a fair and equitable monetary award.

Intestate Succession: WITH CHILDREN—(1) *Real.* Spouse takes ½; children take ½. (2) *Personal.* Same. NO CHILDREN—Spouse takes $200,000 plus ½ of balance; "kindred" takes ½ of residue.

MICHIGAN

Prohibited Marriages: Bigamous marriages are prohibited. No person may marry his or her parent; grandparent; child; grandchild; stepparent; stepchild; stepgrandparent; grandparent's, child's or grandchild's former spouse; niece; nephew; uncle; aunt; sibling; or first cousin. No person may marry a mentally incompetent person or a person with an untreated venereal disease.

Age of Consent: A person 18 years of age or older may consent to marry.

Consent Requirement: A girl age 16 or 17 may marry with the consent of a parent or guardian.

License Requirement: In order to obtain a license to marry, the parties must file with the county clerk a physician's health certificate. The license is valid for 33 days after issuance. At the request of the county clerk, a party may be required to submit a birth certificate or other proof of age.

Common-Law Marriages: Not recognized.

Annulment: Prohibited marriages (i.e., bigamous or incestuous or one party mentally incompetent) are void without the necessity of legal process. A marriage performed while either of the parties was under the age of legal consent is also automatically void unless the parties have subsequently voluntarily cohabited after attaining the age of legal consent. Children born of a void marriage are deemed legitimate. Where validity is questioned, a petition for annulment will be heard.

Theory of Marital Property: Separate.

Property Distribution upon Divorce: The court may give back to either party "the real and personal estate that shall have come to either party by reason of the marriage."

Intestate Succession: WITH CHILDREN—(1) *Real*. Spouse takes $60,000 plus ½ balance; children take residue. (2) *Personal*. Same. NO CHILDREN—Parents receive same share as children.

MINNESOTA

Prohibited Marriages: Marriages between a person and his or her ancestor, descendant, brother, sister, uncle, aunt, first cousin, nephew, or niece, either whole or half blood, are prohibited as incestuous, unless permitted by customs of aborigine cultures. Bigamous marriages are prohibited.

Age of Consent: Every person who is age 18 or older may enter into a valid marriage.

Consent Requirement: A person who is under age 18 but at least 16 years of age may marry with parental consent and after the judge of the juvenile court in which the person resides has approved the application for a marriage license.

License Requirement: Applications for marriage must state the parties' full names, addresses, ages, and address after marriage, and if either party has previously been married. Applications should be filed with the clerk of the county district court. Licenses are issued after five days and are valid for 6 months from the date of issuance.

Common-Law Marriages: Not recognized.

Annulment: Prohibited marriages are void without further legal proceedings.

Theory of Marital Property: Separate.

Property Distribution upon Divorce: Marital property is subject to equitable division, without regard to fault. Nonmarital property is property that is gifted, inherited, acquired prior to marriage, or excluded by valid antenuptial agreement. The court (1) considers the contribution of each spouse to the acquisition of the marital property, including the contribution of each spouse as homemaker; and then (2) may award to either spouse the household goods and furniture of the parties, whether acquired before or after marriage. Property may be excluded by valid antenuptial contract.

Intestate Succession: WITH CHILDREN—(1) *Real.* Spouse has life estate in homestead, with remainder to children. Other real property, spouse takes ½ and one child takes ½. Spouse takes ⅓; two or more children take ⅔. (2) *Personal.* Spouse receives wearing apparel and no more than $6,000 in household goods and no more than $3,000 in other personal property subject to award of property of sentimental value to child; residue to children. NO CHILDREN—All to spouse.

MISSISSIPPI

Prohibited Marriages: Marriages between a man and his grandmother, mother, or stepmother, between a father and his daughter or legally adopted daughter or granddaughter; between a man and his stepsister (when they have the same father) or aunt (his father's or mother's sister); or between first cousins by blood are declared incestuous and void. Also incestuous and void are marriages between a father and his son's widow, between a man and his wife's daughter or his wife's granddaughter, or between a man and his niece by blood. These provisions apply equally to females. Bigamous marriages are also prohibited and deemed void.

Age of Consent: Males 17 years of age or older and females 15 years of age or older may marry without parental consent.

Consent Requirement: Parental consent is required if the male is under 17 years of age or the female is under 15 years of age.

License Requirement: A license, issued by the circuit court clerk, is required. An application for a license must be filed with the circuit court clerk, and the parties must wait 3 days, during which time the application remains on file and open to the public, before a marriage license may be issued. The application may be filed with any circuit court unless the woman is under age 21, in which case the application must be filed in the circuit court of her county of residence. The parties applying for the license must also present a medical certificate stating that the applicants are free from syphilis. The clerk does not have to issue a license if she feels the applicants are drunk or insane, or are imbeciles.

Common-Law Marriages: Not recognized.

Annulment: Grounds for annulment include (1) incurable impotence; (2) wife pregnant by another at time of marriage without husband's knowledge; (3) lack of physical capacity to consummate marriage; (4) consent obtained by fraud, duress, or force; (5) insanity or idiocy; (6) failure to comply with licensing statutes; and (7) incest.

Theory of Marital Property: Separate.

Property Distribution upon Divorce: There is no property distribution state, but the traditional title theory of property has been superseded by a finding in *Jones v. Jones*, 532 So 2d 574 (Miss. 1988) that allowed equitable distribution.

Intestate Succession: WITH CHILDREN—(1) *Real*. Equal shares to spouse and children. Issue of deceased children receive share of parent. (2) *Personal*. Same. NO CHILDREN—Spouse takes all.

MISSOURI

Prohibited Marriages: Marriages between parents and children, including grandparents and grandchildren of every degree; between brothers and sisters of the half or the whole blood; between uncles and nieces or aunts and nephews; between first cousins; and between persons who lack capacity to enter into a marriage contract are presumptively void. Bigamous marriages are also void.

Age of Consent: A person 18 years of age or older may consent to marry.

Consent Requirement: Persons 15 years of age or older but under age 18 may not marry without the consent of a parent or guardian, and such consent must be written and sworn to before an officer authorized to administer oaths. Persons under 15 years of age may marry only with the consent of the circuit or associate circuit court judge of the county where the license is sought.

License Requirement: The license will be issued for good cause shown after a 3-day wait unless reason of such unusual conditions as make the marriage advisable without a waiting period. Licenses are valid for 30 days.

Common-Law Marriages: Not recognized.

Annulment: There is no relevant statutory provision. However, if the following factors are present, the marriage is presumptively void: (1) bigamy or (2) incest.

Theory of Marital Property: Separate.

Property Distribution upon Divorce: Marital property is subject to equitable disposition. The marital property is presumed to include all property acquired after the marriage, whether held individually or in co-ownership, except for inherited or gifted, and the increase in the value of property acquired prior to marriage. The court considers the following factors in dividing marital property; (1) the contribution of each spouse to the acquisition of the marital property, including the contribution of each spouse as homemaker; (2) the value of property set aside to each spouse; (3) custodial arrangements for minor children; and (4) the conduct of the parties during the marriage.

Intestate Succession: WITH CHILDREN—(1) *Real*. Spouse takes $20,000 plus ½; children take residue. (2) *Personal*. Same. NO CHILDREN—Spouse takes $20,000; parents take residue.

MONTANA

Prohibited Marriages: Bigamous marriages and marriages between ancestors and descendants; between brothers and sisters, whether the relationship is by the half or the whole blood; between first cousins; between uncles and nieces or aunts and nephews, whether by half or whole blood, are prohibited. If parties to a prohibited marriage cohabit after the removal of the impediment, they will be deemed as lawfully married as of the date of the removal of the impediment. Children born of an annulled marriage are legitimate.

Age of Consent: A person 18 years of age or older may consent to marry.

Consent Requirement: The district court may issue a marriage license and marriage certificate form to a party age 16 or 17 if there is no parent capable of giving consent or if there was consent given by both parents or the parent having the actual care, custody, and control of the child and is capable of giving consent. A guardian may also consent. As a condition of the order for issuance of a marriage license, the court must require both parties to participate in a period of marriage counseling.

License Requirement: A license issued by the county clerk is required. The marriage license fee is $30.00 and shall be issued upon proof that each party to the marriage will have attained the age of 18 at the time the license is effective or will have attained the age of 16 and has obtained the judicial approval required. In addition, a certificate of the results of any medical examination is required. Each female applicant, unless exempted, shall file with the license issuer a medical certificate from a physician stating that the applicant has been given a standard blood test performed not more than 6 months before the date of issuance of the license. A license to marry becomes effective throughout the state of Montana 3 days after the date of issuance, unless the district court orders that the license is effective when issued, and expires 6 months after it becomes effective.

Common-Law Marriages: Residents can enter into an informal marriage.

Annulment: Grounds for annulment include (1) lack of physical capacity to consummate marriage; (2) consent obtained by fraud, duress, or force; (3) minor married without lawful consent; (4) party lacked mental capacity to consent, including temporary incapacity resulting from drug or alcohol use; and (5) incest.

Theory of Marital Property: Separate.

Property Distribution upon Divorce: The court may equitably divide the property and assets belonging to either or both, however and whenever acquired, without regard to marital misconduct. The court may consider (1) duration of the marriage; (2) prior marriage; (3) antenuptial agreement of the parties; (4) age, health, station, occupation, amount and sources of income, vocational skills, employ- ability, estate, liabilities, and needs of each party; (5) custodial pro- visions; (6) whether apportionment is in lieu of or in addition to maintenance; and (7) the opportunity of each for future acquisition of assets and income. The court may also consider the contribution of a spouse as homemaker.

Intestate Succession: WITH CHILDREN—(1) *Real.* Spouse takes all unless there are children from a prior marriage. In that event, spouse takes ½ if one child; ⅓ if more than one. (2) *Personal.* Same. NO CHILDREN—Spouse takes all.

NEBRASKA

Prohibited Marriages: Bigamous marriages and marriage with men- tally incompetent persons are void and prohibited. Marriages be- tween parents and children, grandparents and grandchildren, brother and sister of the half as well as the whole blood, uncle and niece, and aunt and nephew are also void and prohibited, as are first cousin of whole blood marriages. Children born into a marriage re- lationship that may be annulled are legitimate unless otherwise de- creed by the court. No person afflicted with untreated venereal disease may marry.

Age of Consent: Any person 17 years of age or older may consent to marry.

Consent Requirement: When either party is a minor, the written consent is required of either one of the parents of such minor if the parents are living together, the custodial parent if the parents are living separate and apart, the surviving parent if one of the parents of such minor is deceased, or the guardian, conservator, or person having the legal and actual custody of such minor.

License Requirement: Persons wishing to marry must obtain a li- cense from a county clerk. The license is valid for one year. Before any county judge issues a license, each applicant must file a certificate stating whether the female applicant has laboratory evidence of immunological response to German measles. The certificate is not required if the applicant is over age 50, has had surgical sterilization, or presents laboratory evidence of a prior test declaring her immunity to rubella.

Common-Law Marriages: Not recognized.

Annulment: Grounds for annulment include (1) bigamy; (2) minor married without lawful consent; (3) party lacked mental capacity to consent, including temporary incapacity resulting from drug or alcohol use; (4) incest; (5) incurable mental illness; and (6) marriage by force or fraud.

Theory of Marital Property: Separate.

Property Distribution upon Divorce: The court may order an equitable division of the marital estate.

Intestate Succession: WITH CHILDREN—(1) *Real.* Spouse takes $50,000 plus ½ balance; children take residue. If children are from prior marriage, spouse takes ½; children take ½. (2) *Personal.* Same. NO CHILDREN—Parents take children's share.

NEVADA

Prohibited Marriages: Incestuous marriages and bigamous marriages are void without the necessity of a decree of divorce or annulment or other legal proceeding. Marriages between persons more closely related than second cousins or cousins of half blood are prohibited. Children born of void marriages are legitimate.

Age of Consent: A person 18 years of age or older may consent to marry.

Consent Requirement: Persons at least 16 years of age may marry if they have the consent of either parent or legal guardian. Persons younger than age 16 may marry only if they have the consent of either parent or legal guardian and authorization of the district court. The court will authorize marriages of persons under age 16 in extraordinary circumstances, including but not limited to pregnancy.

License Requirement: Persons wishing to marry must obtain a license from the county clerk of any county in the state. Proof of age may be required, and the license expires in one year.

Common-Law Marriages: Not recognized.

Annulment: Grounds for annulment include (1) fraud, (2) minor married without lawful consent, and (3) party lacked mental capacity to consent. Annulment of marriages contracted, performed, or entered into within the state may be obtained by complaint, under oath, to any district court of the state. A marriage may also be annulled for any cause that is grounds for annulling or declaring a contract void in a court of equity.

Theory of Marital Property: Community.

Property Distribution upon Divorce: Unless there is a premarital agreement, the court will make a just and equitable division of all community property and property held in joint tenancy on or after July 1, 1979. The court may set aside either spouse's property for the support of the other or for the support of the children as deemed just and equitable.

Intestate Succession: WITH CHILDREN—(1) *Real.* Community property, all to spouse. Separate property, spouse ½; child ½. More than one child, spouse takes ⅓, children take ⅔. (2) *Personal.* Same. NO CHILDREN—Spouse, ½ separate property; parents, ½ separate property. If parents are deceased, brothers and sisters and their issue take ½.

NEW HAMPSHIRE

Prohibited Marriages: All marriages between a woman and her father, uncle, son, brother, grandson, nephew, or cousin are incestuous and void. All marriages between a man and his mother, aunt, daughter, sister, granddaughter, niece, or cousin are incestuous and void. Bigamous marriages are also prohibited. Children born of incestuous marriages entered into in New Hampshire are deemed children born out of wedlock. However, if the marriage was entered into and valid in another state, it will be valid in New Hampshire provided the spouses are or become permanent residents of the state. Children born of such marriages are legitimate.

Age of Consent: A person 18 years of age or older may consent to marry.

Consent Requirement: No male under age 14 and no female under age 13 is capable of contracting a valid marriage. Parents may bring a suit to annul the marriage of their minor child who married under 18 years of age. The annulment lies with the discretion of superior court. If special cause exists and minors between the ages of 13 and 18 desire to marry, they and their parents may apply for permission to marry in writing to a justice of superior court or to the judge of probate of the county in which one of them resides.

License Requirement: All persons wishing to marry must first file a notice of intention to marry with the town clerk, who will issue to the applicant a certificate of marriage 3 days thereafter upon proof of age or divorce or death of prior spouse. The certificate, once issued, is valid for 90 days.

Common-Law Marriages: Residents can enter into an informal marriage.

Annulment: A petition for annulment may be filed by a parent or guardian of a minor child. Parties under the age of consent at the time of the marriage may petition for an annulment in superior court unless one of the parties, after arriving at the age of consent, confirmed the marriage.

Theory of Marital Property: Separate.

Property Distribution upon Divorce: The court may order an equitable division of property, regardless of title. The court will consider (1) duration of marriage, (2) age, health, social and economic status, occupation, vocational skills, employability, separate property, amount and sources of income, needs, and liabilities of parties; (3) opportunity for future acquisition of assets and income; (4) need for custodial parent to engage in gainful employment and effect on children; (5) need of custodial parent to occupy the marital residence; (6) actions of either party that contributed to increase or decrease of property owned by either; (7) significant disparity in contributions to marriage, including care of home and children; (8) direct or indirect contribution to education by one party to the other; (9) expectation of retirement or pension rights; (10) tax consequences; (11) value of property allocated by valid prenuptial agreement;

(12) fault of breakdown in marriage; (13) value of any property acquired prior to marriage and property acquired in exchange for property acquired prior to marriage; and (14) value of any property acquired by gift, devise, or descent or any other factor the court finds relevant.

Intestate Succession: WITH CHILDREN—(1) *Real.* Spouse takes $50,000 plus ½ balance; children take residue. If children are from prior marriage, spouse takes ½; children take ½. (2) *Personal.* Same. NO CHILDREN—Spouse takes $50,000 plus ½ balance; parents take residue.

NEW JERSEY

Prohibited Marriages: Bigamous marriages and marriages between ancestors and descendants, between sisters and brothers, aunts and nephews, uncles and nieces, whether of the whole or half blood, are prohibited and void. Children born of void or prohibited marriages are legitimate regardless of the parents' marital status.

Age of Consent: A person 18 years of age or older may consent to marry.

Consent Requirement: Persons under 18 years of age may not marry without the consent of their parents or guardian given in the presence of witnesses. Any person under 16 years of age is required to have such consent approved in writing by either a county judge or any juvenile and domestic relations judge.

License Requirement: A license must be obtained from the licensing officer of the municipality in which the woman resides, in which the man resides if the woman is a nonresident, or in which the marriage will take place if both parties are nonresidents. Before the license will be granted, applicants must present a medical certificate stating they are not infected with syphilis. The marriage license is valid for 30 days after the date of issuance.

Common-Law Marriages: Not recognized.

Annulment: Grounds for annulment include (1) bigamy; (2) lack of physical capacity to consummate marriage; (3) party lacked mental capacity to consent, including temporary incapacity resulting from drug or alcohol use; and (4) incest. Any minor under the age of 18 at the time of marriage may nullify the marriage if he or she has not confirmed it after reaching the age of majority. A marriage may also be annulled if it is allowable under the general equity jurisdiction of superior court.

Theory of Marital Property: Separate.

Property Distribution upon Divorce: The court may make an award to the parties, in addition to alimony, to ensure an equitable distribution of property, both real or personal, that was legally and beneficially acquired during marriage unless by gift, devise, or intestate succession.

Intestate Succession: WITH CHILDREN—(1) *Real.* Spouse takes $50,000 plus ½ balance; children take residue. If children are from prior marriage, spouse takes ½; children take ½. (2) *Personal.* Same. NO CHILDREN—Spouse takes $50,000 plus ½ balance; parents take residue.

NEW MEXICO

Prohibited Marriages: Bigamous marriages and all marriages between relations and children, including grandfathers and grandchildren of all degrees, brothers and sisters of the half or the whole blood, and uncles and nieces or aunts and nephews, are void.

Age of Consent: A person 18 years of age or older may consent to marry.

Consent Requirement: No person under the age of 18 years may marry without the consent of the parent or guardian. No person under the age of 16 years may marry, with or without the consent of a parent or guardian, unless the female is pregnant and the marriage would not be incestuous.

License Requirement: Each couple desiring to marry in New Mexico shall obtain a license from a county clerk and file it for recording.

Common-Law Marriages: Not recognized.

Annulment: Grounds for annulment include (1) minor married without lawful consent and (2) incest. Children born of an annulled marriage are legitimate.

Theory of Marital Property: Community.

Property Distribution upon Divorce: Community property is divided equally.

Intestate Succession: WITH CHILDREN—(1) *Real.* Spouse takes all community and ¼ separate property. Children take ¾ separate property. (2) *Personal.* Same. NO CHILDREN—Spouse takes all.

NEW YORK

Prohibited Marriages: A marriage is void if it is between ancestors and descendants, brothers and sisters of either the whole or half blood, uncle and niece, or aunt and nephew. Bigamous marriages are also void. Children of void marriages are legitimate.

Age of Consent: A person 18 years of age or older may consent to marry.

Consent Requirement: If either party is at least 16 years old but under age 18, he or she may marry with the written and authorized consent of the parent(s) or guardian. A party between the ages of 14 and 16 may marry with the written and authorized consent of a parent(s) or guardian and the written approval and consent of a justice of the court.

License Requirement: Persons wishing to marry must obtain a license from the city clerk. Before the license is issued, parties who are not Caucasian, Indian, or Oriental must have a sickle cell anemia blood test. The license is valid for 60 days.

Common-Law Marriages: Not recognized.

Annulment: Grounds for annulment include (1) bigamy; (2) lack of physical capacity to consummate marriage; (3) consent obtained by fraud, duress, or force; (4) minor married without lawful consent; (5) party lacked mental capacity to consent; and (6) incurable mental illness (for 5 years or more).

Theory of Marital Property: Separate.

Property Distribution upon Divorce: Marital property is subject to equitable distribution. Exempted is property acquired before marriage or by gift or inheritance and personal injury awards. Factors considered are (1) income and property of each party at time of marriage and time of divorce action; (2) duration of marriage, and age and health of parties; (3) need of custodial parent to occupy the marital residence; (4) loss of inheritance or pension rights upon dissolution of the marriage; (5) any award of maintenance; (6) any equitable claim, including joint efforts or expenditures or contributions as homemaker; (7) character of property; (8) probable future financial circumstances; (9) difficulty of evaluating any asset or interest; (10) tax consequences; (11) wasteful dissipation of assets; (12) transfer of assets without fair consideration or any other factor the court finds just and proper.

Intestate Succession: WITH CHILDREN—(1) *Real*. Spouse takes $50,000 plus ½ of balance; children take residue. (2) *Personal*. Same. NO CHILDREN—Spouse takes all.

NORTH CAROLINA

Prohibited Marriages: Bigamous marriages are void, as are marriages between any two persons nearer of kin than first cousins; double first cousins; and a male under age 16 and any female. Also prohibited are marriages in which one or both parties are physically impotent or incapable of contracting marriage from lack of will or understanding. Children born of void or voidable marriages are legitimate.

Age of Consent: A person 18 years of age or older may consent to marry.

Consent Requirement: A person over age 16 and under age 18 must obtain the written consent of either parent if living with both parents, the consent of the custodial parent if the parents are not living together, or the consent of the person, agency, or institution having legal custody or serving as guardian. An unmarried female between the ages of 12 and 18 who is pregnant or has given birth may marry the putative father of the child provided the parties agree and written consent as set out above has been obtained or the consent of the director of social services has been given.

License Requirement: A license, issued by the registrar of deed of the county where the marriage is intended to take place, is required. In order to get a license, the registrar may require the applicants to produce certified copies of their birth certificates or birth registration cards and a certificate executed within 30 days from the date presented that a regularly licensed physician examined the applicants. The license is valid for 60 days from the date issued.

Common-Law Marriages: Not recognized.

Annulment: Grounds for annulment include (1) bigamy, (2) lack of physical capacity to consummate marriage, (3) minor married without lawful consent, (4) party lacked mental capacity to consent, and (5) incest.

Theory of Marital Property: Separate.

Property Distribution upon Divorce: Court shall determine equitable distribution of property. The court considers the following factors: (1) the income, property, and liabilities of each party; (2) obligation of support from a prior marriage; (3) duration of marriage, and age and physical and mental health of parties; (4) need of a parent with custody to own the marital residence; (5) expectation of nonvested pension or retirement rights that are separate property; (6) contribution to the acquisition of the marital property, including the contribution of each spouse as homemaker; (7) any direct or indirect contribution to education or career potential of the other; (8) any direct contribution to an increase in value of separate property during the marriage; (9) the character of all marital property; (10) difficulty of evaluating any asset or interest; (11) tax consequences; (12) acts of either to preserve or dissipate marital property during period after separation and before distribution; and (13) any other factor just and proper.

Intestate Succession: WITH CHILDREN—(1) *Real.* Spouses take ½; child takes ½. More than one child, spouse takes ⅓; children take ⅔. (2) *Personal.* All if under $15,000; if over, ½ to spouse if only one child; ½ to child. More than one child, ⅓ to spouse; ⅔ to children. NO CHILDREN—Spouse takes ½ real property and $25,000 of personal property plus ½ of balance; parents take residue.

NORTH DAKOTA

Prohibited Marriages: Marriages between persons who are intoxicated or under the influence of drugs; marriage by an institutionalized, severely retarded woman under age 45 or a man of any age, unless he marries a woman over the age of 45; and marriages between parent and child, grandparent and grandchild, brother and sister of the half and whole blood, and first cousins of the half and whole blood are prohibited. Children of void marriages are legitimate.

Age of Consent: A person 18 years of age or older may consent to marry.

Consent Requirement: Persons between the ages of 16 and 18 need parental or guardian consent to marry. Persons under 16 years of age may not marry under any circumstances.

License Requirement: Persons wishing to marry must apply to a county judge for the marriage license. The judge shall require the applicants to furnish an affidavit of some disinterested and credible person that the parties are over age 18; if they are under age 18, a certificate of parental or guardian consent signed under oath before a notary public is required. The judge shall also require an affidavit showing whether either party (1) has been divorced; (2) is a habitual criminal; or (3) is under a duty to pay child support or alimony. The applicants must also furnish a physician's certificate showing that neither party is afflicted with syphilis or any other contagious venereal disease. The judge may examine and question witnesses as to the legality of any contemplated marriage. The license is valid for 60 days.

Common-Law Marriages: Not recognized.

Annulment: Grounds for annulment include (1) bigamy; (2) lack of physical capacity to consummate marriage; (3) consent obtained by fraud, duress, or force (unless afterward with full knowledge of the facts, the party cohabited with the other as husband or wife); (4) party is of unsound mind (unless after coming to reason the party freely cohabited with the other as husband or wife); (5) minor married without lawful consent (unless after attaining legal age, the party freely cohabited with the other as husband or wife); and (6) incest. A marriage may be annulled by action in district court.

Theory of Marital Property: Separate.

Property Distribution upon Divorce: The court shall make an equitable distribution of the real and personal property of the parties as they deem just and proper.

Intestate Succession: WITH CHILDREN—(1) *Real.* Spouse takes $50,000 plus ½ balance; children take residue. (2) *Personal.* Same. NO CHILDREN—Parents take children's share.

OHIO

Prohibited Marriages: Bigamous marriages and marriages between parties nearer of kin than second cousins are prohibited. Children born of void or prohibited marriages are legitimate.

Age of Consent: Males 18 years old and females 16 years old may consent to marry.

Consent Requirement: A minor may marry with the consent of his or her parents or guardian or anyone who has been awarded permanent custody of the minor by a juvenile court. However, parental consent is not required if a parent resides in a foreign country, has neglected or abused a minor for 1 year or more, is incompetent, is an inmate of a state mental or penal institution, or has been deprived of custody.

License Requirement: An application for a marriage license is issued by the probate court within the county where either applicant resides or, if neither is a resident of the state, where the marriage is expected to be solemnized. Both parties must personally apply for the license unless a judge is satisfied upon an affidavit of an active and reputable physician that one of the parties is unable to appear in court. In such a case a license may be issued upon the application and oath of the other party; however, the person unable to appear in court must file an affidavit giving the information required for the issuance of a license. If either applicant is under the age of 18, the judge may require them to state that they have received marriage counseling satisfactory to the court. A license will not be issued when either party is under the influence of liquor or a controlled substance or is infected with a communicable form of syphilis. The license, once issued, is valid for 60 days.

Common-Law Marriages: In 1992, Ohio repealed its statute recognizing informal marriages.

Annulment: Grounds for annulment include (1) failure to consummate marriage; (2) bigamy; (3) consent obtained by fraud, duress, or force, unless such party afterwards and with full knowledge of fraud, duress, or force, voluntarily cohabited with the other; (4) party is of unsound mind; and (5) minor married without lawful consent.

Property Division upon Divorce: The division of marital property shall be equal unless such a division is inequitable. Then, the court shall divide it between the parties in an equitable manner.

Intestate Succession: WITH CHILDREN—(1) *Real.* Spouse takes $60,000 plus ½ balance if natural or adoptive parent of child; child takes residue. If not child of marriage; spouse takes $20,000 plus ½ balance; child takes residue. Spouse takes $60,000 plus ⅓ balance if natural or adoptive parent or more than one child; children take residue. If not children of marriage, spouse takes $20,000 plus ⅓ balance; children take residue. With more than one child, spouse takes $30,000 plus ⅓ balance; children take ⅔. (2) *Personal.* Same. NO CHILDREN—Spouse takes all.

OKLAHOMA

Prohibited Marriages: Incestuous and prohibited marriages include marriages between ancestors and descendants of any degree; stepfather and stepdaughter or stepmother and stepson; uncle and niece or aunt and nephew, except in cases where such relationship is only by marriage; siblings of the half or whole blood; and first cousins. However, any marriage of first cousins performed lawfully in another state is valid and binding. Bigamous marriages are also prohibited. The children of void marriages are legitimate.

Age of Consent: An unmarried person 18 years of age or older may consent to marriage with a person of the opposite sex.

Consent Requirement: A person under 18 years of age can marry with the express consent and authority of a parent or guardian. Every person under 16 years of age is expressly prohibited to marry, unless the court authorizes the marriage in settlement of suits for seduction or paternity or unless the unmarried female is pregnant or has given birth to a child. However, the court will not authorize the marriage of males or females under 16 years of age when the unmarried female is pregnant, unless at least one parent, guardian, or custodian of each minor has had an opportunity to be heard and object to the marriage.

License Requirement: A marriage license issued by a judge or the clerk of the district court is required. The license is issued upon written application, signed, and sworn to in person before the judge or clerk by both parties to be married and upon the filing of a certificate or affidavit from a physician licensed by the state, stating that each party has been given a standard serological examination not more than 30 days prior to the application date and that neither party is infected with a communicable state of syphilis. If one or both parties is under the legal age, the application must be on file in the clerk's office for at least 72 hours. The license issued is valid in any county within the state for 30 days.

Common-Law Marriages: Residents can enter into an informal marriage.

Annulment: Grounds for annulment include (1) bigamy, including remarriage within 6 months of a divorce; (2) minor married without lawful consent; and (3) party lacked mental capacity to consent, including temporary incapacity resulting from drug or alcohol use.

Theory of Marital Property: Separate.

Property Distribution upon Divorce: The court will make a just and equitable division of property that has been acquired jointly by the parties. The court may also set aside a portion of the separate estate of a spouse for the other custodial spouse for support of the children. When a divorce is granted, the court will return to each spouse the property owned by him or her before marriage and the undisposed-of property acquired by either spouse in his or her own right during the marriage. Either spouse may be granted alimony out of real or personal property of the other as the court thinks reasonable.

Intestate Succession: WITH CHILDREN—(1) *Real.* Spouse takes ½; children take ½ if issue of surviving spouse. If one or more children are not issue of surviving spouse, spouse takes ½ interest in the property acquired by the joint industry of the husband and wife during coverture and an equal share with the children of the residue.

(2) *Personal.* Same. NO CHILDREN—Spouse takes all property acquired by the joint industry of the husband and wife during coverture and ⅓ in remaining estate; parents take residue.

OREGON

Prohibited Marriages: Bigamous marriages and marriages between first cousins or any nearer relative of the whole or half blood are prohibited. Children of void marriages are legitimate.

Age of Consent: Persons at least 17 years of age may contract to marry.

Consent Requirement: Persons under age 18 may marry with the written consent of the parents or guardian. A license may be granted to persons under 18 years of age if either party has no parent or guardian living in the state and either party to the marriage has resided in the county 6 months prior to filing the application.

License Requirement: Parties wishing to marry must obtain a marriage license from the county clerk. Before the license is issued, the applicants must file with the county clerk an affidavit by some person other than the applicants stating whether the applicants are under age 18, and if so, that they have complied with the consent requirement. The license is effective 3 days after its issuance and is valid for 60 days thereafter. The waiting period may be waived with court permission.

Common-Law Marriages: Not recognized.

Annulment: Grounds for annulment include (1) bigamy; (2) consent obtained by fraud, duress, or force; (3) minor married without lawful consent; (4) party lacked mental capacity to consent, including temporary incapacity resulting from drug or alcohol use; (5) one or both entered into marriage as a jest or dare; and (6) incest.

Theory of Marital Property: Separate.

Property Distribution upon Divorce: The court will make a just and proper distribution of all property held by the parties. The court will consider homemaker contributions. There is also a rebuttable presumption that both spouses have contributed equally to the acquisition of property. Fault in causing the divorce may not be considered.

Intestate Succession: WITH CHILDREN—(1) *Real*. Spouse takes all, unless there are children from a prior marriage. Then, spouse takes ½; children take ½. (2) *Personal*. Same. NO CHILDREN—Spouse takes all.

PENNSYLVANIA

Prohibited Marriages: Bigamous marriages are void. Marriages to an ancestor, descendant, brother, sister, uncle, aunt, niece, nephew, first cousin, the spouse of one's parent or child, or the child or grand-child of one's spouse; marriage to an insane person unless a judge of the orphans' court decides the marriage is in the best interest of the parties and the public; and marriage to a person infected with communicable syphilis are all prohibited.

Age of Consent: A person 18 years of age or older may consent to marry.

Consent Requirement: A person under 18 years of age may marry with the consent of a parent or guardian. Persons under 16 years of age may marry only upon a decision rendered by the orphans' court.

License Requirement: Persons wishing to marry must obtain a license issued by the Court of Common Pleas. A syphilis test is required. There is a 3-day waiting period after applying for the license, except in an emergency or extraordinary circumstances. The license is valid for 60 days.

Common-Law Marriages: Residents may enter into an informal marriage.

Annulment: Grounds for annulment include (1) impotence; (2) bigamy; (3) consent obtained by fraud, duress, or force; (4) minor married without lawful consent; (5) party lacked mental capacity to consent (60-day limit for filing action for temporary incapacity); (6) incest; and (7) a marriage entered into when either of the parties was under the influence of intoxicating drugs or liquor.

Theory of Marital Property: Separate.

Property Distribution upon Divorce: The court will divide the marital property equitably between the parties without regard to marital misconduct after considering the following: (1) length of the marriage; (2) prior marriage; (3) ages, health, station, amount and sources of income, vocational skills, employability, estates, liabilities, and needs; (4) contribution to the education or increased earning power of the other; (5) opportunity for future acquisitions of assets and income; (6) sources of income; (7) contribution (including that of a homemaker) or dissipation to value of property; (8) value of property set apart to each party; (9) standard of living during marriage; (10) economic circumstance of each party, including tax ramifications; and (11) custody of minor children.

Intestate Succession: WITH CHILDREN—(1) *Real*. Spouse takes ½; child takes ½. With more than one child, spouse takes ⅓; children take ⅔. (2) *Personal*. Same. NO CHILDREN—Spouse takes $20,000 plus ½ of balance; parents take residue. If parents are deceased, brothers and sisters and their issue take residue.

RHODE ISLAND

Prohibited Marriages: Bigamous marriages are void. Any marriage where either spouse is an idiot or a lunatic at the time of such marriage is void. Marriages between parents and children, including grandparents and grandchildren of every degree; between sisters and brothers of the half or the whole blood; between uncles and nieces or aunts and nephews; between first cousins; and between stepparents or parents and their children's spouses are prohibited and void. Children born of void marriages are legitimate.

Age of Consent: A person 18 years of age or older may consent to marry.

Consent Requirement: If a female is under 16 years old and a male is under 18 years old, they may marry only with the consent of the Director of Public Welfare. Females between the ages of 16 and 18 may marry only with parental consent.

License Requirement: A marriage license must be obtained from the clerk of the town or city in which the female resides; the town or city in which the male resides, if the female is a nonresident of this state; or the city or town in which the proposed marriage is to be performed if both parties are nonresidents of this state. Persons who have previously been married are required to present a copy of their divorce decree to the town clerk. Before a license is issued, each applicant must file a certificate from a licensed physician. The license is valid for 90 days.

Common-Law Marriages: Residents may enter into an informal marriage.

Annulment: Bigamy is considered grounds for annulment.

Theory of Marital Property: Separate.

Property Distribution upon Divorce: The court may assign to either spouse a portion of the estate of the other. The court uses the following factors to determine the nature and value of the property to be so assigned: (1) length of the marriage; (2) conduct of parties during marriage; (3) contribution of each to acquisition, preservation, or appreciation of respective estates; and (4) contribution of either as a homemaker. The court may not assign property held in the name of one of the parties prior to marriage, but may assign income therefrom resulting from efforts of either spouse. The court may not assign property received by gift from a third party or inheritance.

Intestate Succession: WITH CHILDREN—(1) *Real.* Spouse has life estate in all; children take remainder. (2) *Personal.* Spouse takes ½; children take ½. NO CHILDREN—Spouse takes life estate in real property and $50,000 from personal property plus ½ balance. Parents take residue. If parents are deceased, brothers and sisters and their issue take residue.

SOUTH CAROLINA

Prohibited Marriages: No person may marry his or her parent, grandparent, child, grandchild, sibling, grandparent's spouse, child's spouse, grandchild's spouse, spouse's parent, spouse's grandparent, stepchild, stepgrandchild, sibling's child, or parent's sibling. Bigamous marriages are void, except when a spouse who is presumed to be dead for 7 years is found to be living. Children born of void marriages are legitimate.

Age of Consent: A person over the age of 18 may consent to marry. Proof of age is required of all applicants over age 18 but under age 25.

Consent Requirement: Parental or guardian consent is required when the woman is between the ages of 14 and 18 and the man is between the ages of 16 and 18. Consent of one of the female's parents or of the Superintendent of the Department of Social Services is required for the marriage of a female and male under age 18, who could otherwise enter into a marital contract, when the female is pregnant or has given birth to a child and the male is the putative father.

License Requirement: A license is required for all persons wishing to marry. A written application must be filed with the probate judge (in Darlington and Georgetown counties, with the clerk of the court) at least 24 hours before the marriage license is issued.

Common-Law Marriages: Residents can enter into an informal marriage.

Annulment: Prohibited marriages are void.

Theory of Marital Property: Separate.

Property Distribution upon Divorce: The court may make an equitable apportionment of marital property, defined as all property acquired during the marriage except gifts or inheritances from third parties, property acquired prior to marriage, any increase from such properties not a result of other spouse's efforts, or property excluded by agreement. The court will give weight to the following factors: (1) duration of the marriage; (2) marital misconduct; (3) value of the marital property and each spouse's contribution thereto, including that of homemaker; (4) the income and earning capacity of the parties and opportunity for future acquisitions of capital assets; (5) the health of each spouse; (6) need for training or education to achieve income potential; (7) amount of nonmarital property; (8) vested retirement benefits; (9) award of alimony; (10) desirability of award of the home to spouse with custody; (11) tax consequences; (12) support obligations from a prior marriage; (13) encumbrances on marital property or upon separate property, and debts incurred during marriage; (14) child custody arrangements; and (15) other relevant factors.

Intestate Succession: WITH CHILDREN—(1) *Real.* Spouse takes ½; child takes ½. If more than one child, spouse takes ⅓ and children take ⅔. (2) *Personal.* Same. NO CHILDREN—Spouse takes ½; parents and brothers and sisters or their issue take equal share of residue.

SOUTH DAKOTA

Prohibited Marriages: Marriages between parents and children, ancestors and descendants of every degree, brothers and sisters, half-brothers and half-sisters, uncles and nieces, aunts and nephews, and cousins of the half as well as of the whole blood are null and void. Marriage with a stepchild is null and void. Bigamous marriages are also void. Children of void marriages are legitimate.

Age of Consent: A person 18 years of age or older may consent to marry.

Consent Requirement: A person between the age of 16 and under the age of 18 may marry with the written consent of the parent or guardian. A woman who is pregnant or has given birth to a child may marry at any age without parental consent.

License Requirement: A marriage license must be obtained from the registrar of deeds for a $25.00 fee.

Common-Law Marriages: Not recognized.

Annulment: Grounds for annulment include (1) bigamy, (2) lack of physical capacity to consummate marriage, (3) consent obtained by fraud or force, (4) party is of unsound mind, and (5) minor married without lawful consent.

Theory of Marital Property: Separate.

Property Distribution upon Divorce: The court divides equitably the property belonging to either husband or wife or both, without regard to noneconomic marital fault. The court shall have regard for equity and the circumstances of the parties.

Intestate Succession: WITH CHILDREN—(1) *Real.* Spouse takes ½; child takes ½. If more than one child, spouse takes ⅓ and children take ⅔. (2) *Personal.* Same. NO CHILDREN—Spouses take first

$100,000 plus ½ of balance; parents take residue. If parents are deceased, brothers and sisters and their issue take residue.

TENNESSEE

Prohibited Marriages: Bigamous marriages are prohibited. Also prohibited are marriages between lineal ancestors or descendants or lineal ancestors or descendants of a parent, or with the child of a grandparent, the lineal descendants of a husband or wife, or the husband or wife of a parent or a lineal descendant.

Age of Consent: A person 18 years of age or older may consent to marry.

Consent Requirement: A person 16 or 17 years of age may marry with parental, next of kin, or guardian consent, sworn under oath.

License Requirement: Persons wishing to marry must obtain a license from the clerk of the county where the woman resides or where the marriage ceremony is to be performed. The license is valid for 30 days thereafter. A premarital physical examination is required before a marriage license is issued. No license will be issued to drunks, insane persons, or imbeciles.

Common-Law Marriages: Not recognized.

Annulment: There is no relevant statutory provision, but the following factors are grounds for annulment in case law: (1) failure to consummate marriage, (2) bigamy, (3) habitual intemperance, (4) party is of unsound mind, and (5) incest.

Theory of Marital Property: Separate.

Property Distribution upon Divorce: Marital property, which includes increase in separate property through joint efforts but exempts inherited or gifted property, is distributed by the court in equitable proportions without regard to fault. Factors in decision include (1) duration of the marriage; (2) age, physical and mental health, vocational skills, employability, earning capacity, financial needs, and liabilities of the parties; (3) contributions, both tangible and intangible, to education, training, or increasing earning power of one spouse to another; (4) ability for future acquisition of income and assets; (5) contribution of each to acquisition, preservation, appreciation, or dissipation of the marital or separate property, including contribution as homemaker, wage earner, or parent; (6) value of separate property; (7) estate at time of the marriage; (8) parties' relative economic position and earning power; and (9) tax consequences.

Intestate Succession: WITH CHILDREN—(1) *Real.* Equal shares to spouse and children, but spouse must take at least ⅓. (2) *Personal.* Same. NO CHILDREN—Spouse takes all.

TEXAS

Prohibited Marriages: A person may not marry an ancestor or descendant by blood or adoption, a brother or sister of the whole or half blood or by adoption, a parent's brother or sister of the whole or half blood, or a son or daughter of a brother or sister of the whole or half blood or by adoption. Bigamous marriages are void.

Age of Consent: A person 18 years of age or older may consent to marry.

Consent Requirement: A male or female 14 to 18 years of age may marry with the written consent of a parent or guardian, or a minor may petition the court in their own name for permission to marry.

License Requirement: Persons wishing to marry must first obtain a license from the county clerk with proof of age. The marriage license is valid for the 30 days following a 72-hour waiting period.

Common-Law Marriages: Residents can enter into an informal marriage.

Annulment: Grounds for annulment include (1) lack of physical capacity to consummate marriage; (2) consent obtained by fraud, duress, or force; (3) minor married without lawful consent; (4) party lacked mental capacity to consent, including temporary incapacity resulting from drug or alcohol use; and (5) one party divorcing another party 30 days before the wedding without informing his or her new spouse.

Theory of Marital Property: Community.

Property Distribution upon Divorce: The court divides community property as it deems just and right.

Intestate Succession: WITH CHILDREN—(1) *Real.* Surviving spouse owns ½ community in own right; receives ½ interest in surviving spouse's ½ community; receives a life estate in separate property; children take residue and remainder. (2) *Personal.* Surviving spouse owns ½ community in own right; receives ½ interest in surviving spouse's ½ community; takes ⅓ separate property; children take residue. NO CHILDREN—Spouse takes all community property, all separate personal property, and ½ separate real property; parents take ½ separate real property. If parents are deceased, brothers and sisters and their children take ½ separate real property.

UTAH

Prohibited Marriages: Marriages between parents and children, ancestors and descendants of every degree, brothers and sisters of the half or the whole blood, uncles and nieces, aunts and nephews, or first cousins, or between any persons related to each other within but not including the fifth degree of consanguinity, are void. Marriage to a person with AIDS, communicable syphilis or gonorrhea, to a person of the same sex, or to a person under 18 years of age if consent is not obtained is prohibited. Bigamous marriages and remarriages before a divorce is absolute are also prohibited and void, as is the marriage of any person under the age of 14 years. Children born of void marriages are legitimate.

Age of Consent: A person 18 years of age or older may consent to marry.

Consent Requirement: A person under age 18 but over 14 years of age may marry with the consent of his or her father, mother, or guardian, given in person to the court clerk, or in writing, signed and acknowledged before a person authorized to administer oaths.

License Requirement: A license issued by the county clerk is required. The license is valid for 30 days from issuance. If the county clerk does not know the parties personally, one of them must swear and file an affidavit showing that there is no lawful reason to stop the marriage.

Common-Law Marriages: Residents can enter into an informal marriage.

Annulment: A marriage may be annulled when the marriage is prohibited or there are other grounds existing at common law.

Theory of Marital Property: Separate.

Property Distribution upon Divorce: The court will divide the property equitably.

Intestate Succession: WITH CHILDREN—(1) *Real*. Spouse takes all unless there are children from a prior marriage; then, spouse takes ½; children take ½. (2) *Personal*. Same. NO CHILDREN—Spouse takes all.

VERMONT

Prohibited Marriages: Men and women are prohibited from marrying their parents, grandparents, children, grandchildren, siblings, siblings' children, aunts, and uncles. All marriages void because of incest or bigamy do not require a decree of divorce or other legal process to declare their nullity.

Age of Consent: A person 18 years of age or older may consent to marry.

Consent Requirement: Persons under age 18 may marry with written parental or guardian consent. Persons under age 16 need the previously mentioned consent in addition to a certificate from a probate, district, or superior judge certifying that the public good requires the license to be issued. No person under age 14 may marry.

License Requirement: Persons wishing to marry must obtain a license from a town clerk. At least one of the parties to the proposed marriage must sign the certifying application as to the accuracy of the facts supplied by the applicants. The license shall be issued by the clerk of the town where either the bride or groom resides or, if neither is a resident of the state, by a town clerk in the county where the marriage is to be solemnized.

Common-Law Marriages: Not recognized.

Annulment: Marriages prohibited by law are void without legal process.

Theory of Marital Property: Separate.

Property Distribution upon Divorce: The court will equitably divide and assign all property owned by either or both of the parties, however and whenever acquired. The court will consider (1) length of the marriage; (2) age and health of the parties; (3) the occupation, source, and amount of income of each of the parties; (4) vocational skills and employability; (5) contribution by one spouse to the education, training, or increased earning power of the other; (6) value of all property interests, liability, and needs of each party; (7) whether in addition to or in lieu of alimony; (8) opportunity of each for further acquisition of assets and income; (9) desirability of awarding family home to the spouse with custody of children; (10) party through whom the property was acquired; and (11) the contribution of each spouse to acquisition, preservation, and depreciation or appreciation of value of estate, including contribution of homemaker; (12) respective merits of the parties.

Intestate Succession: WITH CHILDREN—(1) *Real.* Spouse takes ½; child takes ½. If more than one child, spouse takes ⅓; children take ⅔. (2) *Personal.* Spouse takes all clothing and ornaments; children take residue. NO CHILDREN—Spouse takes $25,000 plus ½ of balance; parents take residue in equal shares. If parents are deceased, brothers and sisters or their issue take residue.

VIRGINIA

Prohibited Marriages: Bigamous marriages are absolutely void. Marriages between an ancestor and a descendant, a brother and a sister, an uncle and a niece, or an aunt and a nephew, whether the relationship is by the half or the whole blood, are prohibited. Marriages between parties under the age of 18 contracted without the required consent, and marriages in which one party lacks the capacity to consent to marriage because of mental infirmity, are void. Marriages between persons of the same sex are also prohibited.

Age of Consent: A person who is 18 years of age or older may consent to marry.

Consent Requirement: Persons under age 18 may marry with parental or guardian consent or, when parental or guardian consent cannot be obtained because the parties are orphans or have been

abandoned, with the consent of the judge of the circuit court of the
county or city where either party resides.

License Requirement: The license for a marriage shall be issued by
the clerk of the circuit court of the county or city in which either of
the parties resides. The license is valid for 60 days from the date of
issuance. Persons empowered to issue marriage licenses shall at the
time of issuing the license provide the applicants with information
concerning genetic disorders and a list of family planning clinics located in the county or city of the issuing office.

Common-Law Marriages: Not recognized.

Annulment: Grounds for annulment include (1) impotence; (2) wife
pregnant by another at time of marriage without husband's knowledge; (3) conviction of a felony (before the marriage and without the
knowledge of the other party); (4) bigamy; (5) consent obtained by
fraud, duress, or force; (6) minor married without lawful consent;
(7) party lacked mental capacity to consent (including temporary
incapacity resulting from drug or alcohol use); and (8) incest.

   Also, if either party had been a prostitute before the marriage
and without the knowledge of the other, or if the man fathered a
child born to a woman other than his wife within 10 months after
the solemnization of the marriage, the marriage may be annulled.

Theory of Marital Property: Separate.

Property Distribution upon Divorce: Virginia has a unique law that
classifies some property as separate and some as marital and some
as both separate and marital. Separate property is all property acquired before marriage, by gift or inheritance. Income received from
separate property is separate if not attributable to the personal effort of either spouse or to marital property. Marital property is
property titled in the names of both parties or any property not
defined as separate. Pension and retirement funds are presumed to
be marital. Part separate property and part marital property includes the income from separate property attributable to the efforts
of one of the spouses; property that is commingled; personal injury
or workers' compensation awards; or retitled property. The non-
owning spouse has the burden to prove that property should be
classified as marital property. The court will consider (1) the contributions, monetary and nonmonetary, of each party to the well-

being of the family; (2) the contributions, monetary and nonmonetary, of each party in the acquisition and care and maintenance of such marital property of the parties; (3) the duration of the marriage; (4) the ages and physical and mental conditions of the parties; (5) the circumstances that contributed to the divorce; (6) how and when property was acquired; (7) the debts and liabilities of each spouse and the basis of these debts; (8) the liquid and nonliquid character of the property; (9) tax consequences; (10) any other factors necessary to arrive at a fair and equitable award.

Intestate Succession: WITH CHILDREN—(1) *Real.* Spouse takes all unless children from prior marriage; then, wife takes dower or curtesy rights; children take remainder. (2) *Personal.* Same. NO CHILDREN—Spouse takes all.

WASHINGTON

Prohibited Marriages: Marriages between persons under 17 years of age are void without court permission. Bigamous marriage and marriages between parties closer than second cousins, whether of the whole or half blood, are prohibited. Marriages between a man and his father's sister, mother's sister, daughter, sister, son's daughter, daughter's daughter, brother's daughter, or sister's daughter and marriages between a woman and her father's mother, mother's brother, son, brother, son's son, daughter's son, brother's son, or sister's son are prohibited. Children of void marriages are legitimate.

Age of Consent: A person 18 years of age or older may consent to marry. Upon a showing of necessity, this age requirement may be waived by a superior court judge of the county in which one of the parties resides.

Consent Requirement: Persons 17 years of age may marry with written parental or guardian consent, in the form of an affidavit sworn to and subscribed before a person authorized to administer oaths.

License Requirement: Persons wishing to marry must obtain a license from the county auditor of the county where they intend to marry. Before issuing the license, the county auditor will require the applicants to make and file an affidavit showing that they are not afflicted with any contagious venereal disease.

Common-Law Marriages: Not recognized.

Annulment: Grounds for annulment include (1) bigamy; (2) minor married without lawful consent; (3) party lacked mental capacity to consent, including temporary incapacity resulting from drug or alcohol use; (4) incest; and (5) failure to ratify the marriage by voluntary cohabitation after attaining the age or capacity to consent or after cessation or discovery of force or duress.

Theory of Marital Property: Community.

Property Distribution upon Divorce: Court may dispose of assets in a just and equitable manner without regard to marital misconduct. The factors they may consider in their disposition are (1) the nature and extent of the community property, (2) the nature and extent of the separate property, (3) the duration of the marriage, (4) the economic circumstances of each spouse at the time the division becomes effective, including the desirability of awarding the family home or right to live there to the spouse with custody of the children.

Intestate Succession: WITH CHILDREN—(1) *Real.* Spouse takes all community property, ½ separate; children take ½ residue. (2) *Personal.* Same. NO CHILDREN—Spouse takes community plus ¾ separate; parents take residue.

WEST VIRGINIA

Prohibited Marriages: Men and women are prohibited from marrying their parents, grandparents, siblings, children, grandchildren, half-siblings, aunts, uncles, nieces, nephews, first cousins, and double cousins. If the relationship was created by adoption, such marriages are permitted. Children of void marriages are legitimate.

Age of Consent: Persons 18 years of age or older may consent to marry.

Consent Requirement: Persons under age 18 may marry with the written consent of a parent or legal guardian having custody of the minor at the time the application for a marriage license is made. No person under the age of 16 may be issued a license except upon order of the circuit judge and with the consent of a parent or guardian.

License Requirement: Persons wishing to marry must obtain a license from the clerk of the county commission in which either party usually resides. Where both parties are nonresidents of the state, the license will be issued by the clerk of the county commission in which the application is made. Before any license is issued, each applicant must file a certificate, from a physician duly licensed by the state, stating that the named party is not infected with syphilis. In cases of emergency or extraordinary circumstances, a judge of any court of record may waive the requirement of a physician's certificate and may direct the clerk of the court to issue the license. The license is valid for 60 days upon its issuance.

Common-Law Marriages: Not recognized.

Annulment: Grounds for annulment include (1) impotence, (2) wife pregnant by another at time of marriage without husband's knowledge (or had been a prostitute), (3) bigamy, (4) commission and/or conviction of an infamous crime (conviction prior to marriage), (5) force or fraud, (6) party is of unsound mind, (7) minor married without lawful consent, (8) incest, and (9) one party suffers from a venereal disease unknown to the other. If the husband was "notoriously licentious" before the marriage without the wife's knowledge, this also constitutes grounds for an annulment.

Theory of Marital Property: Separate.

Property Distribution upon Divorce: Marital property is defined as all property acquired during marriage, regardless of ownership, and the increase in the value of separate property that results from the use of marital property funds, or any work performed by either during the marriage. Separate property is property acquired during marriage by gift or inheritance and any increase due to conditions outside the control of the parties. Unless there is a valid agreement, the court will divide marital property equally, but may consider (1) the extent each has contributed to the value of the marital property, including employment income, separate property, homemaker services, child care services, and labor in a family business; (2) the extent to which the efforts of one spouse have limited or decreased the other's earning power; and (3) the extent to which one party may have dissipated or depreciated the value of the marital property.

Intestate Succession: WITH CHILDREN—(1) *Real.* Children take all. (2) *Personal.* Spouse takes ⅓; children take ⅔. NO CHILDREN— Spouse takes all.

WISCONSIN

Prohibited Marriages: Bigamous marriages are prohibited, as are marriages between persons who are nearer of kin than second cousins. However, a marriage between first cousins where the female is age 55 or where either party, at the time of the application for a marriage license, submits an affidavit signed by a physician stating that either party is permanently sterile is not unlawful. A divorced person may not marry again until 6 months after the judgment of divorce was granted.

Age of Consent: A person 18 years of age or older may consent to marry if otherwise competent.

Consent Requirement: If a person is between the ages of 16 and 18 years, a marriage license may be issued with the written consent of parent, guardian, or custodian. If there is no parent, guardian, or custodian or if the custodian is a state agency or department, the written consent may be obtained from the court after notice to the agency or department.

License Requirement: A marriage license must be obtained from the county clerk of the county in which one of the parties has resided for at least 30 days immediately prior to making the application. If both parties are nonresidents of the state, the marriage license may be obtained from the county clerk of the county where the marriage ceremony is to be performed. The license is valid for 30 days after issuance. It will be issued within 5 days of application.

Common-Law Marriages: Not recognized.

Annulment: Grounds for annulment include (1) lack of physical capacity to consummate marriage; (2) minor married without lawful consent; (3) party lacked mental capacity to consent, including temporary incapacity resulting from drug or alcohol use; or (4) any marriage prohibited by law.

Theory of Marital Property: Community.

Property Distribution upon Divorce: The Uniform Marital Property Act (UMPA) was enacted effective January 1, 1986. This established a modified community property system. There is a presumption that all property is marital property and each spouse has an undivided one-half interest in this property. Property brought into the marriage or acquired after marriage by gift or inheritance is individual property, but the income from this property is marital property. Individual property commingled with marital property becomes marital property unless it can be shown otherwise. Both spouses may participate in the management and control of the marital property if they act together.

Intestate Succession: WITH CHILDREN—(1) *Real.* Spouse takes all unless children from prior marriage. Then, spouse takes ½; children take ½. (2) *Personal.* Same. NO CHILDREN—Spouse takes all.

WYOMING

Prohibited Marriages: Bigamous marriages, marriages involving mental incompetents, and marriages between parties who stand in relation to each other of parent and child, grandparent and grandchild, brother and sister of the half or whole blood, uncle and niece, aunt and nephew, or first cousins are prohibited. Also prohibited are marriages between persons below the age of consent who failed to get the required consent. Children born of void marriages are legitimate.

Age of Consent: A person age 16 or over may contract to marry.

Consent Requirement: A marriage between persons under 16 years of age is prohibited and voidable unless before contracting to the marriage a judge approves the marriage and authorizes the county clerk to issue a license. When either party is a minor, no license shall be granted without the verbal consent, if present, and written consent if absent, of the father, mother, guardian, or person having the care and control of the minor.

License Requirement: A license from the county clerk is required. Upon receipt of the application, the county clerk shall ascertain, by the testimony of a competent witness and the applicant, the names,

residences, and ages of the parties and whether there is any legal
impediment to the marriage. Each female under age 45 shall file a
certificate reciting that she has received a test for rubella and Rh
blood type. Should the clerk refuse to issue a license because of the
applicants' failure to comply with any of the requirements for its
issuance, application can be made to a judge of the district court,
who can order the clerk to issue the license. If either applicant is
under 16 years of age, the parents or guardian may apply to any
judge of a court of record in the county of residence of the minor
for an order authorizing the issuance of the marriage license.

Common-Law Marriages: Not recognized.

Annulment: Grounds for annulment include (1) bigamy; (2) minor
married without lawful consent; (3) party lacked mental capacity to
consent, including temporary incapacity resulting from drug or alcohol use; and (4) incest.

Theory of Marital Property: Separate.

Property Distribution upon Divorce: In granting a divorce, the court
shall make such disposition of the property of the parties as appears
just and equitable, considering the condition in which the parties
will be left by the divorce, the party through whom the property
was acquired, and the burdens imposed upon the property for the
benefit of either party and children.

Intestate Succession: WITH CHILDREN—(1) *Real.* Spouse takes ½;
children take ½. (2) *Personal.* Same. NO CHILDREN—Spouse takes
all.

APPENDIX B:
WRITTEN EXAM

Make two photocopies of this exam, one for you and one for your partner. Answer the following questions based on the laws in your state as listed in Appendix A. If your answer to any numbered question is yes, proceed to the next section of the question.

1. What is the age of consent for marriage in your state? _____

2. Are common-law marriages recognized in your state? _____

3. Are you related to your future spouse in any way? _____
   a. If your answer is yes, is your marriage prohibited in your state? _____

4. Are you currently serving in the Armed Forces of the United States _____
   a. If your answer is yes, determine if your military status will interfere with your new marital status. _____

5. Have you been married before? _____
   a. If your answer is yes, do you have final divorce papers from your prior marriage? _____
   b. If your answer is yes, determine if there is a waiting period before you may remarry and if you have complied with the waiting period. _____

6. Is there any physical or mental reason why you could not legally marry based on the laws of your state? _____
   a. If your answer is yes, consult an attorney in your home state regarding your concerns. _____

7. What are the grounds for annulment in your state? _____

8. What theory of marital property ownership does your state recognize? _____

9. What assets are considered nonmarital property by your state? _____

10. What is the difference between tenants in common and joint tenants who own real estate? _____

11. Do you currently have life, health, auto, or other insurance? ____
   a. If your answer is yes, have you consulted your insurance agent to determine how you can combine coverage or change beneficiaries on your policies? _____

12. Do you currently have a company pension plan? _____
   a. If your answer is yes, have you added your spouse to the plan? _____

13. Have you notified Social Security of your marriage? _____

14. What are the federal tax ramifications of your upcoming marriage? If you don't know, consult an accountant and then answer the question. _____

15. Will the date of your marriage have an impact on taxes owed? If you don't know, consult an accountant and then answer the question. _____

16. Do you currently have a valid will? _____
   a. If your answer is yes, take steps to add your spouse and/or determine if the will remains valid after your marriage. ____

17. If you died without a valid will, how would your state divide your estate? _____

(If the answer to question 16 was no and you don't like the answer to question 17, talk to an attorney about preparing your last will and testament. If you don't have an attorney, follow the steps in chapter 6 and compare the prices and qualifications of three attorneys before choosing one to represent you.)

18. Did you prepare a list of assets and debts, as suggested at the beginning of chapter 6? _____
   a. If your answer is yes, go to the next question. _____
   b. If your answer is no, follow the instructions in chapter 6 and prepare a list before proceeding with this exam. _____

19. Do you have any assets, or foresee any income from assets, you would like to keep separate from the marital estate? _____
   a. If your answer is yes, make a list of those assets. _____

20. Do you have business interests you plan to keep separate from the marital estate? _____
   a. If your answer is yes, make a list of those assets. _____

21. Is there any need to protect marital assets from any premarital debts on your list? _____
   a. If your answer is yes, make a list of those debts. _____

22. Are there any issues raised by other family members that would indicate that a written agreement might be advisable to protect both yourself and your future spouse at a later date?
_____
   a. If your answer is yes, make a list of those issues. _____

(If your answer is yes to any one of questions 19 through 22, consider a premarital agreement.)

If you and your spouse are marrying for the first time, congratulations! Now, exchange checklists and study your partner's answers. A comparison of answers and potential issues will allow you to head off any potential problems before they arise. The marriage laws were written for couples who are young and who are about to marry for the first and last time. Good luck!

If either you or your spouse are remarrying, please continue and answer the following questions:

24. Do you receive any benefits as a result of a prior marriage, such as alimony, social security benefits, pensions, or medical insurance? _____
    a. If your answer is yes, have you researched the impact of a remarriage on your continued ability to receive such benefits? _____

25. Have you considered the financial impact of obligations to former spouses on your new relationship? _____

26. Do either you or your partner have children from prior relationships? (The questions that follow might apply to your situation if you have dependents other than minor children.) If the answer is yes, address the following concerns:
    a. Have you made trustee and/or guardianship arrangements for children in your last will and testament? _____
    b. Have you and your partner discussed the issue of stepparent adoption? _____
    c. Have you resolved any heirship issues between a prior family and your new spouse by executing a valid will? _____
    d. Have you and your partner discussed the impact on your marital finances of current child support obligations? _____
    e. Have you investigated the impact of a new spouse's income on the eligibility for financial aid of college-age children from a prior marriage? _____

If either you or your new spouse is nearing age 55, please continue and answer the following questions:

27. Has either of you taken advantage of the one-time exclusion of $125,000 from income taxes on the sale of a home? (Be aware that if one spouse has taken the exclusion on a home the other is barred from that exclusion in the future. Consider the impact of the sale of your homes *before* the ceremony.) _____

GLOSSARY

Age of consent: The age at which a person may legally enter into a marriage contract without the consent of a parent or guardian (also used to denote the age at which a woman may consent to sexual intercourse).

Alimony: A money allowance made to a wife by court order from a husband's estate, either during or after divorce. During the pendency of a divorce, the proper term is alimony pendente lite.

Annulment: To legally void something. As applied to marriage, the law looks upon the relationship as having never existed.

Appellate court: A court that reviews appeals from lower courts and either affirms, reverses, or modifies the decision.

Attainder: Loss of civil rights as a result of a felony conviction.

Beneficiary: One who receives the proceeds of an estate or insurance policy.

Bigamy: The crime committed when a person enters into a second marriage without dissolving the first.

Cohabitation: Legally, to live as husband and wife.

Common law: The body of law that originated in England (1) in contrast to the civil law of Rome, (2) in contrast to the equity of the chancery courts of England, and (3) as distinguished from ecclesiastical laws of the church. Today, in Anglo-American jurisdictions, common law is distinguished from laws created by statute.

Common-law, or informal, marriage: Generally, a marriage created by an agreement to marry, followed by cohabitation and a public recognition of the relationship as a marriage, in contrast to a ceremonial marriage.

Community property: Property owned by a husband and wife in common, with each owning an undivided one-half interest by reason of their marital status.

Consanguinity: A relationship that exists because of a common ancestor or descendant.

Consideration: An inducement offered and accepted in order to form a contract.

Consortium: The conjugal fellowship of husband and wife, including the right to the company, cooperation, and aid of the other. The term is used in tort actions as a right that carries compensatory damages to one spouse for the injury or death of the other.

Contract: A promise, or set of promises, either oral or written, either implied or express.

Court: A Governmental body that administers justice.

Curtesy: A common law right given to a husband that allows him to enjoy a deceased wife's estate during his lifetime.

Devise: The act of giving property in a last will and testament.

Dissolution: The cancellation of a contract or the ending of a marriage in divorce.

Divorce: The judicial dissolution of a marriage.

Domicile: A person's fixed residence.

Dower: The interest of a wife in a deceased husband's estate during her lifetime.

Duress: Compulsion by threat or force that forces a person to do something against their will.

Equal protection: A phrase in the Fourteenth Amendment to the Constitution of the United States in a passage that requires the states to extend equal treatment and protection to all persons under its laws. Unequal treatment is unconstitutional.

Equity: That which is just and fair; a system of law that corrects failures of justice.

Fraud: A conscious act of deceit or misrepresentation.

Gift: The voluntary transfer of property without consideration.

Heir: A person who inherits property either under a valid will or by operation of the laws of intestate succession.

Incest: The crime of sexual intercourse between a man and woman whose marriage is prohibited by law.

Intestate: The legal state of dying without a valid will.

Issue: A direct descendant.

Joint tenants: Tenants who have one and the same interest in land, arising from one and the same conveyance, beginning at the same time, and held in the same, undivided possession.

Last will and testament: The term arises from the division in ecclesiastical court and common law courts in medieval times. *Will* is the Anglo-Saxon word and *testament* comes from Latin. The two terms arose because the church had jurisdiction over personal property and the state over real property. Today, common usage of the term describes an instrument that seeks to devise all property after death.

Life estate: An interest in property held by a party for their, or someone else's, lifetime.

Misrepresentation: Words or conduct that mislead a party, particularly in connection with execution of a contract.

Necessaries: Material things that are indispensable for the sustenance of life. There is significant flexibility in the definition, depending on the financial situation of the parties.

Putative spouse: A reputed spouse unaware of a legal impediment to a marriage.

Residue: Portion of an estate that remains after all debts and specific bequests have been made.

Separate property: Property owned by a married person in his or her own right during marriage. In a community property state, separate property would be defined as property acquired before marriage or after marriage by inheritance or gift.

Tenants in common: Tenants who hold the same land but whose interests might arise under different titles and in distinct shares.

Tort: A civil wrong. Torts include such actions as personal injury claims arising out of auto accidents, workers' compensation claims, and the like.

Undue influence: Influence exerted that induces a party to act against their will.

Void marriage: A marriage with no legal force or effect.

Voidable marriage: A marriage that is technically invalid but may be made valid by an act of the parties in the future.

Wrongful death: Laws that provide, after the death of a person, recovery for damages by his or her heirs, enacted by every state to override the common law rule that the death of an individual did not give rise to a cause of action in a civil suit.

INDEX

Property (*cont.*)
  and quickie divorces, 20
  separate vs. community, 5
  and "tenants in common" or
      joint tenants, 46–47
  title to, 45, 46–47
  and wife, 118
  and voided marriage, 25
  See also Community prop-
      erty; Separate property;
      and specific states
Putative spouse, 213
  protections for, 25

Q

"Quasi-community" property,
    43–44

R

Race, 13, 18
Rape, 108
Real estate
  owned before marriage, 48
  and property laws, 43, 46
  records file, 77
Records, 38, 77–78, 120
Reimbursement, and commu-
    nity property laws, 39
Relatives, 16–17
Remarriage, 4
  and bigamy laws, 19–20
  and estate planning, 65
  and fiscal issues, 51, 52, 59–
      62
  and marital contract, 80, 86,
      89–93
  rates, 132
  trends, 136, 138
Remuneration for services, 85–
    86

Rental properties, 90
Reproductive rights, 122–123
Residency, legal, 6, 112–113
Residue, 214
Responsiblity for acts of child,
    124–125
Retirement accounts, 66, 75
Retirement benefits. See Pen-
    sion plans and retire-
    ment benefits
Revocable trusts, 73–74
Reynolds vs. United States, 20
Rhode Island, 28, 82, 191–192
Rights, 105
  to inherit, 68, 123
    and stepparent adoptions,
        128
  of married women, 84
  to marry, 11–24
  to sue for loss of consortium,
      6
Rooney, Mickey, 79
Running for political office, 113

S

Safe-deposit box, 78
Same-sex marriage, 4, 13, 19,
    123, 139
Savings, 53
  and child rearing, 120
  and estate planning, 66
  and marital contract, 87, 95
  systematic, 62
School activities, 13
Self-employment taxes, 57
Senior citizens, 4
Separate property, 5
  commingled with community
      property, 38–39, 44–45
  vs. community property